The Ballast Seed

A Story of Motherhood, of Growing Up and Growing Plants

ROSIE KINCHEN

WEIDENFELD & NICOLSON

First published in Great Britain in 2022 by Weidenfeld & Nicolson,
an imprint of The Orion Publishing Group Ltd
Carmelite House, 50 Victoria Embankment
London EC4Y 0DZ

An Hachette UK Company

1 3 5 7 9 10 8 6 4 2

A CIP catalogue record for this book is
available from the British Library.

ISBN (Hardback) 978 1 4746 1817 5
ISBN (eBook) 978 1 4746 1819 9
ISBN (Audio) 978 1 4746 1841 0

Typeset by Input Data Services Ltd, Somerset

Printed and bound in Great Britain by Clays Ltd, Elcograf S.p.A.

www.weidenfeldandnicolson.co.uk
www.orionbooks.co.uk

Contents

For my mother, and for my sons

Ballast Seeds

. . . at the end of the last Ice Age, the British Isles were home to only a handful of plants . . . The majority of these introductions (the plants that came later) occurred over two centuries between 1735–1935

Sue Shephard, *Seeds of Fortune*, 2003

Plants have travelled the world for as long as we have, but never more so than in the eighteenth and nineteenth centuries, when ships navigated the globe carrying rum, sugar, cotton and spice. As well as their cargo, these trade vessels carried ballast – earth, stone and gravel that was used to weigh the ship down when it docked. In among this ballast were seeds, tiny stowaways hitching a ride from port to port. These seeds remained dormant until the ballast was dumped on heaps outside harbours – often clandestinely, in order to avoid taxes. Then they began to grow. It is impossible to say how many plant species were introduced to Britain in this way, but records of the time show that ballast heaps were thriving habitats. Some of these newcomers would have lasted a season, never surviving beyond the first frost. Others found that our temperate climate suited them and they naturalised, quietly changing the countryside. Some are still lying there, waiting for the right conditions in which to grow.

Prologue

Propagation: noun
1. *the breeding of specimens of a plant or animal by natural processes from the parent stock.*
2. *the action of widely spreading and promoting an idea, theory, etc.*

For a long time, I assumed that growing up happened in a linear pattern: that you built up to adulthood at a steady and manageable pace, like hiking up a mountainside; you trudge on through the challenging parts, moving forwards at a brisk but satisfying pace. Perhaps for some people it does happen this way, but for me that was not the case.

This is a book about the moment when the path beneath me began to shift and I lost my footing completely. It was not composed, it was not comfortable, and it caught me completely unprepared. I think that a similar thing can take place at key moments in life – divorce, bereavement, loss. It happened to me when I was supposed to be at my happiest. I had one healthy, happy son, and discovered that somehow (we are still not quite sure about the how part) another was on the way.

I didn't feel euphoric or blessed or any of the other sentiments you see embossed on the front of a greetings cards. I felt ambushed. As though an invisible enemy had shoved me off the edge of a cliff. I couldn't justify or rationalise the feeling, so I had to find a way to make peace with it instead.

This is a book about what happened next. It is about the uncomfortable consequences of motherhood: selfishness and ambition, frustration and fear, and the tidal wave of shame that very nearly engulfed me altogether. I don't offer solutions, simply because I don't really have any. This is not a self-help guide: I have no messages about persevering, about scaling back or leaning in.

It is a book about surviving, about wading through quicksand with a newborn and, finally, deliriously reaching the other side. It is also about finding comfort in the least promising places: in the dusty, dirty corners of the city, in the plants that grow there, in the sow thistles that guard the pavement like soldiers and the ivy that cloaks the city's walls.

I noticed them for the first time, and went on to discover their stories and find a thread linking me back through the centuries to all the others who have called London their home. It is also a story about friendship: the people who find their way to you and then change the way you see the world.

Marianne North was an aristocratic adventuress and botanical artist — not an obvious source of comfort, not least because she had been dead for over a hundred years. But her impatience and frustration with the world chimed with mine, and she took me by the wrist and frogmarched me through Chilean peaks and the jungles of Brazil. She taught me about power and prejudice, about avarice and greed. Most of all, she taught me about plants: how to notice them, how to learn from them. She showed me the eternal joy of making things grow.

I

Glacialis: The Month of Ice

The baby was born was born two weeks before Christmas. Tinsel hung on the walls of the operating theatre and in the background the radio played. As he was lifted from my womb, the opening chords of East 17's 'Stay Another Day' rang out. I would have objected on his behalf, demanded a more dignified soundtrack for his entrance into the world, but I was, at that moment, quite sure that I was going to be sick.

The caesarean delivery had been my choice. It would be simpler, I thought. I would be in hospital on a set date and a grandparent could be summoned in advance to take care of the toddler at home. Perhaps I would feel psychologically stronger and better prepared to manage the punishing weeks ahead. I realised as I was wheeled into the operating theatre, hairnet on and recycled cardboard sick bowl in my hand, that this may not pan out as intended. I had never expected childbirth to be a transcendental experience; I wasn't interested in doulas or whale music. I had watched one hypno-birthing video early in my first pregnancy, tried hard to visualise my inner goddess as instructed and swiftly gone for a massage instead. For me labour was an ordeal, something to grit my teeth and get on with, like an eight-mile run or a bad bout of food poisoning.

But this time the day felt off-kilter from the start. There was a backlog of surgeries to get through and I had been nil by mouth for fifteen hours by the time I made it to the front of the queue. The baby communicated his irritation in the only way he could, a frantic volley of kicks that pulled my stomach from side to side like a tent in a gale. Dimly I worried about the wilderness beyond, in the unwaxed, untended half of my body that I had not seen for months. P and I sat together in the waiting room in silence, observing the people around us as though they were part of an anthropological experiment. There was a young blonde with a shell-shocked expression, who I imagined must be having her first child. Her partner hovered anxiously around her as she clasped the arms of the waiting-room chair. 'Can I get you some water?', 'Some ice?', 'Shall I text your mum?' he buzzed.

The other couple were harder to read: a woman a little older than I was and a man who turned up later in exercise kit, as though he was casually stopping in on his way to a spin class. I listened to their stilted conversation wondering whether it was the ambivalence of familiarity or something more interesting. Was he a one-night stand who was staying the course? A supportive friend stepping in at her hour of need? The game amused me until I turned the lens on us: my pale, swollen face and P's tired gaze, the silence between us, oppressive and uncomfortable, brought it to a stop.

Both couples went in before we did. But finally, as the not-quite-a-person in my belly bellowed for breakfast, it was our turn. I was wheeled into the operating room. The anaesthetist and the doctor were young men, fresh-faced students who looked like extras in a daytime medical drama. I was their twelfth caesarean delivery that day, they told me, the metallic tinkle of tools sounding their hurry to get on. As I was manoeuvred back on to the cold surgical trolley, I listened to them discussing the hospital nativity play; one of them had been cast as Mary and needed to borrow a nightdress for the role. I seemed to have become surplus to the plot just as the drama reached its climax. There was nothing for me to do but take a deep breath and close my eyes.

The pressure had been mounting inside my head for months, a cold feeling of dread running through my veins as my stomach grew. The pregnancy had come as a shock at a time in my life when the last thing I wanted were surprises. It had taken three months for me to realise what was happening even though, with hindsight, the signs were staggeringly clear.

My taste for alcohol disappeared overnight. My favourite white wine developed an acid flavour that transported me straight back to the pubs of my teens, when I drank booze not *for* the taste but despite it. I crawled home from work in the evenings, feeling dazed and hungover, only to fall asleep the moment the toddler went to bed. Eventually I dug out an old pregnancy test from the bottom of the bathroom drawer, only to reassure myself that the barely audible voice in the back of my head was wrong. The test was positive, but even then I wouldn't believe it. I sat on the toilet and scrutinised the box, reading every word of the small print, until I found some evidence of a flaw.

There it was: a sell-by date and we were well beyond it. I chucked it into the bin, enjoying a flicker of frustration as I set off to work. But now the hint of doubt was getting louder and harder to ignore. By the end of the day it had grown into something more like panic. I picked up three more tests on my way home, took them up to the bathroom, leaving the toddler in front of the TV, and stared as lines appeared on each of those as well. I don't know how long I sat there, gripping the edge of the bath, sifting through the chaos in my head. I felt disorientated, dizzy.

There was an undercurrent of euphoria as well, as though some future version of myself was looking back at this moment and laughing at the drama taking place below. But very quickly worry set in. I had a one-year-old to take care of and a career which was in a critical condition. My relationship with P was more strained than it had ever been and our finances were non-existent. I didn't have the strength to consider what this would mean. Rushed calculations followed as I tried to figure out when this could have happened, cursing my own inability to do simple maths in my head.

I heard P outside the bathroom door, trying to coax the toddler into his pyjamas as he got ready for bed, and cast around one final time for a reason to delay. Then I walked into the bedroom and told him, watching as the panic I was feeling spread across his face as well. To his credit, he composed himself quickly. 'How do you feel?' he asked. 'Tired. Happy,' I said, already aware that it wasn't entirely true.

As the weeks passed, P's enthusiasm grew. 'We were going to have another one anyway; why not now?' he said. I knew he was right. My misgivings were probably just hormonal, I told myself, the anxiety would steady and the slump would fade.

But the feeling of unease only intensified as the pregnancy progressed. When I had been pregnant with my first child such a short time ago, the excitement had been too much to bear. It had taken all the strength I could muster not to announce it to everyone I knew well before I reached the twelve-week mark. This time the opposite was happening. I tried to imagine telling our friends and family, running through the dialogue that was still so fresh from the year before, but this time I couldn't deliver the performance I knew would be expected of me. There would be jokes and laughter: 'You two didn't hang about!' How would I hide my cold, creeping dread?

As the pressure mounted, I began to cry compulsively – in Pret at lunchtime as fat tears soaked my cheese and pickle baguette, on the bus home. I started wearing sunglasses to spare my fellow commuters the discomfort of watching a pregnant woman weep. It was at the office that the feeling was most intense. I had returned to work from maternity leave less than a year beforehand, assuming that my career would resume more as it had been before. Instead, the dynamics seemed to have changed completely: team members had been hired, my responsibilities had shifted. I told myself that I was imagining it, that a period of readjustment was normal, and I'd be able to reorientate myself quickly enough.

I said yes to everything, determined not to give anyone an opportunity to think that I was less competent, less able in any way. Yes I could interview a TV presenter at a private members' club at 8 p.m., no it didn't matter that I would be missing bedtime. Yes I could fly to Madrid to interview an actress. I watched her in a one-woman show leaping about on stage pretending to be an amoeba, and wondered how P and the toddler were managing at home.

He had quietly taken on more and more of our domestic life so that I could keep up the charge, but the change had created an unspoken wound between us. We had never discussed the division of labour when we were starting a family; it went without saying that we would split it equally. But here we were, barely out of the starting blocks, and that ideal had collapsed already; biology was non-negotiable, my career had been upended by our baby and his had not. I tried to suppress my irritation, but the injustice of it stung me. Of course women left the workplace when they started families, but I had let myself believe that it was their choice.

The second pregnancy sounded the death knell for my career; I knew it from the moment I saw the second line on the test. My response was denial. I sat at my desk, gorging on berries to quell the sugar cravings and immersed myself in the job. I spoke to people with real problems: an author with cancer, a woman whose husband was in prison in the Emirates suspected of being a spy, quietly relieved by the temporary distraction they offered from my own self-pity.

But it didn't last. Whenever I was alone – usually in bed or on the bus – the panic flared up and my head began to throb again. I told my boss only when baggy cardigans and unbuttoned trousers would no longer hide the bump. He was dumbstruck but delighted; a tricky management situation solved just like that.

Almost immediately I felt myself beginning to fade. A female editor mentioned in passing that she'd sent someone else to do an interview I'd been wanting to do for months. 'It was in New York and you're not going to want to fly,' she said. A week later, my boss brought a new colleague in to introduce to the team. He went around the desks, giving our names and job titles until he reached me. 'You don't need to worry about Rosie, she's off on maternity leave,' he said. It felt like I was being physically pushed out of the door.

Gradually I began to welcome this invisibility. My favourite winter coat, a pop of fuchsia pink that cheered up the greyest winter days, started to feel absurd. I put it away and retreated into a dark-green parka with a fur hood that I could pull round my face.

Startled now, P persuaded me to visit my GP and reluctantly I went, weeping throughout the appointment as the young male doctor looked awkwardly at his notes. 'What would you like me to do?' he said when I finished talking, and once more I could hear that shadow version of myself laughing at the absurdity of it all.

He suggested I try antidepressants which he was 'fairly sure' wouldn't hurt the baby. It was a risk I didn't feel I could take. Instead I embarked on NHS talk therapies, awkward phone conversations with faceless strangers. I lost track of how many medical professionals asked if I had had suicidal thoughts. I shook my head and wondered if anyone having suicidal thoughts ever said yes.

I was well aware that what was happening was irrational. Close friends were going through the grim ritual of IVF, the excruciating cycle of hope, grief and loss while everybody else talked about their plans for their summer and what to eat for dinner that night. Others were still single, confident women in their mid-thirties used to calling the shots, now hanging in a limbo of uncertainty while their fertility raced off into the horizon.

My course was set already; what was the problem? I could see the intractable logic of this argument, but it seemed to make no difference at all. Panic morphed into terror; I knew with absolute certainty that something fundamental was going wrong. I turned down the offer of a sicknote and dragged myself to the office every day, determined that I couldn't afford not to. I tried to write but my brain refused to focus. The effort of getting through each day was all-consuming. Conversations were exhausting and the perpetual blare of the news channels on television too loud.

Maternity leave hovered on the horizon like a finishing line, and I hoped that when I crossed it things would start to improve, that away from the frantic pace of the office my mind would heal itself. But nothing changed. I sat in the baby's room folding and unfolding clothes, flicking through name books and scrolling through photographs of the toddler's early days trying to recapture the rush of love and excitement I'd felt. The person in the pictures felt like someone else entirely. I made half-hearted efforts to prepare the toddler for his brother's arrival. I found a noisy book at the library, a story about Pirate Pete and his new baby brother. I turned the sticky pages, pressed buttons that triggered the wailing of a baby and shut my eyes so that I wouldn't start to cry.

Around me, the inevitable buzz that accompanied a new life grew louder. My parents were oblivious to my distress. I made excuses to avoid meeting up with them and went out of my way to give the impression that all was well. I didn't have the energy to talk about what was happening and I wouldn't have known what to say. Fortunately, they were about to embark on the latest chapter of their retirement adventures. To date they had been on a cruise to Dubrovnik and a coach tour along the Great Wall of China. Now they were off to Australia for three months around the time the baby was due. My mother pinballed between excitement and guilt at missing the arrival of her latest grandchild. She sent me screenshots of the weather forecast in Sydney one moment and emergency contact numbers for relatives who might be able to step in the next. In truth, I was relieved they were going.

All my energy was channelled into maintaining an appearance of normality while inside the building blocks of my personality turned to dust. It reminded me of a construction site we used to drive past on the way out of London. The Regency façade stood immaculate, a cream-cake vision of scrollwork and columns propped up by scaffolding while just inside wrecking balls knocked down the supporting walls one by one.

Only P could see some of the damage. He followed me to the bathroom, where I spent the nights curled up on the floor weeping. I sent him back to bed again. One of us needed to be functioning for the toddler's sake. Besides, this wasn't a rational grief; it was an ever-changing mass, a swarm of insects following me around the house.

In the back of my mind was the uneasy sense that I might have brought this on myself. I had delayed motherhood for as long as possible, not because I didn't want to have a child but because of a persistent suspicion that it wasn't the right job for me. I was impatient and easily bored, qualities I tended to blame on an itinerant childhood. We had moved around the world because of my father's job. Home had been a glass box on the twenty-seventh floor of a New York high-rise, a bullet-proof bunker in the Middle East, a red-brick box in a suburban cul-de-sac here in the UK. None of them had lasted for long enough for me to feel embarrassed by the posters of boys Blu-Tacked to the wall or to discover that my feet now stuck out of the end of the bed.

It sounded exciting, but the reality was something more complicated: a restless feeling that came from not quite belonging in any one place. To confuse things further, my father's family had roots in Ireland and my mother had come to England in a boat from Sri Lanka, stopping over for a couple of years in Pakistan. We grew up hearing stories about crocodiles in the garden and snakes under the bed. She was British enough to take her own tea bags with her whenever she went abroad, but not so British that she didn't tut as she rubbed sunblock into my inconveniently fair skin.

My own ethnicity was all the more baffling because there wasn't much left of it to see. My brother and sister had inherited my mother's dark complexion. I had not. I was the white baby. The English one. There were times when I enjoyed the anarchic rebellion of our genes, the way my family gleefully upended those ethnicity boxes on official forms. And there were other times – when friends' parents assumed that my mother was being paid to pick me up from school – when I wasn't so sure.

I was English, I knew that. But when people asked me where I was from, I had no idea what to say. All of this faded into the background when I moved to London in my twenties, the capital was my first real home and I set to work constructing the foundations of something that resembled a life. But while friends got married in quick succession, it turned out that there was only one real love in my life and that was my career.

I was spellbound the first time I walked into a newsroom. It was a parallel universe where red-faced hacks bellowed instructions and volleys of swearing rang through the air like gunfire.

It was less an office than a battlefield, a world I had read about in the pages of Evelyn Waugh, where not fitting in anywhere else was the best qualification for the job. I loved the topsy-turvy chaos of it all, that phone conversations were conducted in code, rain dripped from the ceiling into strategically placed bins and mice raced between the desks as though they too were eager to read the day's news. The building shook with the sound of constant grumbling, but no one could ever bring themselves to leave.

The job itself was whatever I wanted it to be. I interviewed Julian Assange in the Ecuadorian Embassy; got stuck in a police kettle with a group of masked anarchists; took my clothes off on stage in the name of feminism. I once tracked down the world's most intelligent chimpanzee with the same zeal I would have used to find Lord Lucan and felt just as triumphant when I found her (obviously, she was female).

The rest of my life slotted in around the demands of the work. I moved to different corners of the capital, bewildered by the tribal allegiances people formed to particular postcodes. Men came and went again, usually when they realised that in my life deadlines would always come before dinner.

Loneliness hovered in my peripheral vision, but I blocked it out with a constant stream of noise. I saw friends, went out drinking, lay in bed until noon at the weekends. I bought plants – herbs from the supermarket, gaudy splashes of colour in a metallic bucket, because it didn't really matter if they died or not. It was adulthood-lite and I liked it that way; or that's what I told myself as I sat in front of the TV on my own on a Sunday night.

By the time I met P I was thirty-two years old and starting to wonder if the rush of news was really enough to sustain me forever. We met in a pub where his friend was having a drink with mine. He was hopelessly awkward and impossibly kind. The sort of man I might not have noticed ten years before. I liked his quiet certainty, the way he knew what mattered and seemed to be able to filter out everything else. For the first time I began to imagine a different sort of future: after-school snacks, the yellowing pages of well-thumbed photo albums, holidays on shingle beaches in the drizzle of an English summer. Neither of us wanted to get married; we were each as ambitious as the other and had no plans to slow down. Babies would be a bonus, I assured the girls when we finally got together for lunch at the pub. There would be compromises, of course, but this domesticity would be an added extra, which we would somehow squeeze in like sticky toffee pudding after a long Sunday lunch.

We set out to find a home, traipsing around flats we could not afford in areas that everybody wanted to live in. Outside the cosy bubble of our fledgling romance, the world was moving in ways no one could predict and the property market ground to a halt. I scoured auctions for a doer-upper at a price we could afford, turning up outside houses that had become squats, peering through bay windows and trying to imagine a world I hadn't even considered until a few months before. My growing belly warned us that time was running out. And then, months before my due date, when it felt like we had seen every house in London, we finally found our home.

It was a ridiculous mess of a building. A nineteenth-century coach house with two bedrooms that looked like it had been glued together from bits of leftover beams and bricks, an elaborate crest bonded on to the front for good measure. The front door opened directly on to a double yellow line. It was eccentric, uniquely English and the sort of home I never thought I would live in, let alone own. There were obvious drawbacks. Instead of a garden it had a tiny, shady courtyard overrun with ivy and, P laughed, there wasn't one right angle in the place. But, standing outside in the autumn rain, as my son kicked me with the precision of a metronome, I felt light-headed: so this was where real life would start.

Everything about the move felt symbolic. We packed up the relics of P's bachelor life from the tiny attic flat in north London – a guitar, a surfboard, a box of old mobile-phone handsets, chucking them on a heap like a funeral pyre. I folded up the sparkly shift dresses that I could no longer squeeze over my growing hips, the colourful lingerie and ostrich-feather cape which already felt like ludicrous remnants of a past life. We were completely unprepared for the gear change; there was no dinner service or silverware of the sort our parents would have put on their wedding lists. Instead we had mix-and-match crockery most of it from Ikea, an odd selection of mugs – awkward mementos from past loves – and two chairs.

The only things that did fit into our new house were my plants: a little gaggle of survivors who, despite neglect and total ignorance, I had not yet managed to kill. I unpacked them first and dotted them around the windowsills and empty shelves of the coach house, on top of the biggest boxes that it would take us months to unpack. It was a token gesture, a small way of feathering the nest as I waited for the show to begin.

Now I walked around it in a daze and wondered how I could have been so foolish; of course that vision had to come at a cost. The slide backwards had started as soon as I returned to work. The further back I felt myself falling, the more angry and irritable I became. But the worst of the fury I saved for myself. I had believed that this was possible, that not only would I manage working motherhood, but I would enjoy it; I'd read the empowering books by high-flying career women, I'd interviewed the authors, so why was I now falling flat on my face?

It wasn't simply the emotional demands ahead that scared me but the practical side as well. Two full-time jobs plus two children in full-time care left us staring over a financial precipice. My position as the higher earner, until this point, been a point of pride. After all I was a modern woman, raised on a diet of Sylvia Plath and Margaret Atwood. This was social progress in action. Now the responsibility kept me awake at night. I lay in bed, feeling the baby's kicks, and racked my brain for a solution. And somewhere inside me a knot was forming. A sadness so intense that I couldn't put it into words: the feeling that this new life meant the end of an old one, that I was about to be buried alive.

It was in the middle of this that I found out I was being sent to Tangier to write a travel piece for the newspaper. The trip would fall over my birthday weekend and P decided it would do me good. We left the baby with his grandmother and the rabbit and the houseplants in the care of the next-door neighbour's teenage son. The trip was a mistake. Tangier throbbed with life and energy, the streets were lapis-blue and the air thick with saltwater and hashish. Relieved of the duties of parenthood, the demons grew louder and my head began to pound. I retreated to bed and cried for two days straight. I remember nothing of the journey home, but the sight that greeted us when we got there haunts me still. Every pot was full to the brim. Every plant soggy and submerged. There were puddles of water on the ground, on shelves and on top of cupboards. Our plant-sitter had been watering diligently from the moment our plane took off to the moment we landed.

The devastation felt tragi-comic; of course I was being punished with a flood. Now, as I waited listlessly for the delivery date, I found myself surveying the sodden pots of soil. The yellowing leaves and calcifying branches felt like a quiet sort of crisis: devastation unfolding at a glacial pace. Since the disaster most had slipped into a slow decline and the house had begun to resemble a field hospital. I began to inspect them properly for the very first time. There was a kumquat tree whose leaves had dropped one by one so that only one green branch remained, sticking out jauntily like a bandaged arm. Research suggested it had been 'traumatised', but with the right care and attention it could be nurtured back to health. I trimmed off the dead wood and watched it hopefully for signs of new growth. The aloe had been given to me by an elderly neighbour who lived next door to the central London flat I shared with a girlfriend; she asked me to care for it when she went on holiday and let me keep it when she saw how proud I was of having kept it alive. Now its spiky arms were soft and doughy. I gave the soil a chance to dry out and moved it into a new pot. I had fallen in love with orchids as a student; I felt they were mysterious and faintly exotic – very me. It was about the same time that I had started to smoke menthol slims and read poetry by Baudelaire, apparently unaware of how insufferable I was.

The challenge I had was keeping them alive. I spritzed and misted and soaked, and one by one they died, forcing me to traipse back to the supermarket and splash out and start all over again. My love for these flowers had never faded, but I could still kill them with aplomb. At the time of the flood I had two: a splendid pink one that had been given to me as a house-warming gift and another which had seduced me at the supermarket check-out, where it had been placed deliberately like a siren to charm passers-by.

Now their leaves had turned yellow and their roots were rotting. The larger one was beyond salvation. I threw it in the bin and moved the other to the upstairs bathroom, which, for reasons I couldn't fathom, seemed to work as a sort of orchid intensive care. The cactus I could not part with. It was the first plant P and I had bought together, weeks after I had moved into his flat, tucked away in the rafters above a pet shop called the Mutz Nutz. It was an unfeasibly small space for an unfeasibly tall man, devoid of cushions or curtains. Plants would make it feel like a home, I insisted, herding him off to the garden centre. He walked around, bored, until he saw it – seven feet high and thinner than he was; it was love at first sight.

I realised how impractical it was much later, when I watched as three builders tried to manoeuvre it down the stairs with the help of some picnic blankets and thick gardening gloves. Or later still, when the toddler took his first, unsteady steps and I had to cushion it in bubble wrap to stop him impaling himself on its spikes. Now it looked miserable. I ran my hand over a brown patch the size of fifty-pence piece and wondered how I could stop it spreading.

As the hours inched by, I did everything I could to avoid leaving the house. I retreated more and more often to my bedroom, biting back tears, the toddler watching solemnly, trying to understand what could be happening through his fledgling knowledge of the world. We had recently started a new childcare arrangement, our fifth in just over a year. Miraculously it seemed to be working, and the issue of what we would do about the toddler when I was off work with the baby hung in the air between P and me. Eventually, he suggested that we divert my maternity pay into maintaining the status quo. It was a luxury we couldn't afford, particularly now with my career prospects in tatters, but it would give me space to fix the glitch in my brain. I was as grateful that the option existed as I was ashamed that I needed it at all.

The pregnancy, meanwhile, entered its final stages. The midwife warned me to expect less movement as the due date approached; there would no longer be enough room for the baby to stretch and move. But I found the opposite was true: I woke in the night to kicks and punches, to wriggles and somersaults. This baby was bursting to enter the world just as I was trying to retreat from it.

'OK,' I said at last, heaving myself up from the sofa where Netflix was playing on a loop. 'If you want to walk, we'll walk.' By now all items of clothing with buttons or zips been consigned to a storage bag and shoved under a bed. Instead I wrapped myself in a huge shawl, black and shapeless, the closest thing to an invisibility cloak that I could find, and trudged off to my nearest park. There is nothing remarkable about this patch of green; it isn't a Royal Park that tourists flock to; there are no pergolas opened by kings or queens or domestic staff walking Shih Tzus around decorative ponds. It is next to one of London's biggest teaching hospitals, sandwiched between a train line and a maze of terraced houses.

I made my way uphill to the southern end of the park where, on a clear day, I could look out across the city. I stopped and saw the high-rise estates and old gas holders that surrounded my home, the glass monoliths in the distance, all the way to the edge of the Thames, where the steel rim of the London Eye stared back at me. Joggers ran past stamping out the stresses of the day on the pavement beneath them, dog walkers told off their charges in the indulgent tones of a mother chastising a recalcitrant child. In the centre of the park was a Victorian bandstand, once a point of civic pride, now where a homeless man threw crumbs to the squirrels. I felt calm for the first time in months.

Halfway up the hillside was a small tree I had never noticed before. It was decked out like a carnival float; hearts hung from its branches and its trunk wore a skirt of multicoloured ribbons. I made my way over and stood beneath the canopy, reading the messages written on the satin in indelible ink, each one a 'Rest in peace', an 'I'll never forget you', a tribute to three lost friends. I wondered who they were and why this tree had been chosen as their memorial.

The hospital called on a Thursday morning a week before the baby was due and said that they had a space on the surgical list and would like to bring the operation forward. I sat down on the sofa and took a deep breath, trying to suppress the acid that suddenly surged up my throat. It was happening and I still didn't know how I felt. Then I called P. 'The toddler's coming down with something. The house is a mess. What do you think?' He assured me that there was no harm in saying no. An hour later they called back: 'I'm afraid you have no choice, we've got too many surgeries to get through next week. Yours has been moved to tomorrow morning.' So that was it; our boy was on his way.

The day got off to a terrible start. The toddler had a viral infection. He lay limply on the sofa and refused to take off his pyjamas while his grandmother tried to feed him toast. We made the short walk to the hospital in silence, each of us running through a mental checklist for the one vital thing we would have forgotten to do. Then we took our seats in the same ward I had left, euphoric, a short time before.

The whole day had a strong sense of déjà vu. I remembered the week I had spent pacing the corridors of the maternity wing, feeling the dead weight of my first child pushing downwards, as I waited for the artificial hormones to make their way through my veins and the contractions to start. They never did. That child had been as reluctant to make his debut as this one was eager. I had waited, savouring the delicious agony like a child counting down to Christmas. The last member of my NCT class whizzed past me in the labour ward and came back again babe in arms, delirious with tiredness and excitement. I cried and asked P if I would be pregnant forever. Eventually my baby was nudged out of me by an all-female medical team, wailing crossly as though he had been woken from the most delicious nap.

This time round it was brutal. The old incision had healed, and the surgeons had to cut through a thick layer of scar tissue. I groaned as a wave of nausea consumed me and tried to ignore the feeling that my stomach was being pushed up into my ribs as the sound of machinery filled the room. P hovered beside me with a sick bowl. I gripped his hand and willed him silently to make the whole thing stop. Finally my son's first cry rang out, an angry shriek containing all the horror and the wonder of the world, and moments later he was thrust into my arms, a tiny mass of skin and bone who'd found his way into my womb and clung on through the turbulence and the tears. He looked up at me with enormous eyes and I felt a rush of pure, unfiltered love.

2

Regelationis: The Month of Thawing

It was the middle of the night and I lay in bed feeling the adrenaline surge through my veins. The baby slept in the bassinet beside me, twitching and moaning like a dog chasing rabbits through his dreams. I willed my heart to stop pounding, holding my breath in case the sound would wake him.

Time had slipped its mooring in the days since his birth. The nights bumped into days and weeks disappeared altogether. P returned to work and the toddler slid back into his old routine, leaving the baby and I to get to know one another, strangers in a biologically arranged marriage. He was different outside the womb to the way he had been inside, frail and timid in a way I would never have predicted. The person who had grown within me had been imperious in his demands for food, for room, for life. So sure, in fact, that he had absorbed all my certainty and left a vacuum behind.

Now that he was here, the world seemed to terrify him. He shied away from noise and light, clinging on to me as though he wanted to be anywhere but here. I had not been able to hold him straight after the birth. The midwives laid him on my chest, but the knot of wires and surgical sheets made the embrace feel awkward, as though we were holding hands through a pair of gloves. P tried again a little later, passing him to me so that he could take photographs, but again the nausea overwhelmed me. I groaned and gave him back again. He lay safely in the plastic cot beside me, where I could admire the perfect arc of his lip and his neat little nose. He was beautiful, I could see that straight away, but impossibly fragile, a porcelain figurine to be kept on a shelf and admired but not touched.

Only his hands were strong, disarmingly so; they were big and solid, his father's hands, the kind you could trust. It was P who comforted him through his first night on earth, pacing the corridors of the hospital rocking and patting, assuring him that it would all work out in the end, while I lay in bed, grateful for the catheter and the stitches that kept me there. The toddler's birth had been terrifyingly new and yet completely unsurprising – the final stroke of a painting we'd been working on for months. The moment I held him in my arms I was desperate to get back home again. To carry him over the threshold into his new life; to lie between my own sheets and feel clean in the way you only ever can in your own house. This time I did not want to leave the safety of the maternity ward.

The noise here was comforting: the cries, the moans, the delighted relatives greeting a new branch of the family tree. Even the reassuring beep of heart monitors helped me sleep at night. All of it was a distraction from the dread. It reminded me of the summer I had spent sleeping on a friend's sofa in Soho, reeling from the end of some student fling. I thought I'd use the flat as a base from which to explore the city. Instead I spent the summer glued to the window watching the furtive kisses, the drunken rows, the excitement of other people's lives unfurling on street below.

Now I liked listening to the midwives issuing their orders, fair and firm, the sort of parents we all hoped we would be. It wasn't just the baby who had left my body during the surgery; a part of my mind seemed to have removed itself as well. It floated above, observing with interest as my body tried to heal: I watched the blood pouring out of me; the curls of crimson liquid and jet-black tissue were the physical manifestation of everything I had been feeling for the past months. I hoped I would leave the hospital lighter, purer, purged of the weight I had been carrying around as the baby grew.

It ended, as we knew it had to. Two days after the birth my stitches had healed sufficiently for me to stand without feeling that the world was tipping me over again. The baby and I were both examined one final time and sent home with a large bag of painkillers and a box of syringes for the injections which P would need to administer to stop my blood from clotting. I wrapped up the baby and gingerly we made our way home, discussing tactics as we inched our way into the car and set off. We had been warned that the first time he met his brother would be key and had bought a small plastic construction vehicle to soften the blow.

But the toddler was more concerned with punishing his parents for their absence than with the new sibling we brought home. He inspected him briefly and then lost interest, turning to us with cool disdain. He was angry with us for deserting him in his hour of need. P made him something to eat while he contemplated us in solemn fury, a pudgy emperor deciding our fate with a flick of the thumb. I sat on the sofa and held the baby in my arms, breathing in the smell of biscuits and washing powder as I tried to rally myself for the weeks ahead. It would be all right now,

I reasoned, cradling him in my arms. We'd made it through the hard part.

At first things did seem to improve. The emotional bumps and jolts of pregnancy calmed. The tears stopped as suddenly as they had started. I was back at the wheel again, and surprised to find that I knew what I was doing; the patting of a tiny back, and endless washing of bottles felt like things I'd always done. I sent photographs to friends and family, realised with a jolt that I was pulling out the same babygrows that I had only just folded and put away. But something else changed too. At first, I couldn't work out what it was. I was functioning better than expected. I changed nappies, folded tiny white vests, loaded and unloaded the washing machine, lulled by the mindlessness of it all. But when I picked up the baby I felt numb.

Community midwives came to visit, motherly types who cooed and clucked, weighing and fussing like the myriad aunties of my childhood, people who seemed entirely comfortable in this realm of squalling infants and leaking nipples, and I played along. I looked at the scales, I talked about latches and asked about tied tongues, but it was the baby who was their patient; I was background noise. While they filled in the blank spaces in his little red book, I carried out a self-assessment of my own: I was absent, bored, listless, but I couldn't say with any confidence if anything was actually wrong.

Out of the blue I had a visit from the hospital's psychiatric team; presumably there was a red flag on my file and they were following it up. While the toddler played, a kind woman with a furrowed expression sat in my sitting room and asked about hallucinations, politely enquiring about violent urges towards my own child. I sipped my tea and shook my head. 'No,' I told her and smiled. I didn't have the energy to explain the mass of shifting darkness that had settled over me, or even to try to make sense of it myself. I was not happy. I was not sad. I wasn't really there at all.

The one thing my brain could still do was panic, and since the birth the future had taken on monstrous dimensions in my head. We had just about enough money to last us through the months of maternity leave, but what would happen after that? In theory I still had a job to go back to; I hadn't been sacked, not yet in any case, but I became convinced that it was only a matter of time. I ran over it all, the problems, the rows, the injustice. It felt as though my career had turned into an enormous game of snakes and ladders and every path led me back to the starting point.

The bone-aching exhaustion of life with a newborn permeated my thoughts and turned them into a heaving mass of dread. P asked me how I was feeling. I gave one-word answers and went to bed, leaving him to begin his shift. Somehow, I had forgotten the brutal loneliness of the first weeks of parenthood, the terrifying responsibility of being nightwatchman for a new life. I thought about calling one of the girls. My university friends who had moved to London with me were not geographically far away, but parenthood had created a different sort of distance, one that none of us had expected when we peeled ourselves out of bed, hungover, to talk away whole weekends, a few years before.

Now there was too much ground to cover ever to get round to the things that mattered the most, and I no longer had the energy to try. Shortly afterwards a more pressing issue took hold. I could not get the baby to feed. He screamed for food and then pulled away from my breast, twisting and turning like he was being tortured by the very thing he needed to keep him alive. The toddler had been a big baby from the start, a mass of rolls and dimples that reminded me of a contented Buddha. He took so much pleasure in his food that I worried about how I would ever be able to provide him with enough of it. The baby was at the very opposite end of the scale. He was tiny, with hollow cheeks and frightened eyes, clinging on to me like an infant orangutan in a nature documentary. He was hungry, there was no mistaking that. His screams were so powerful that I couldn't believe they really came from his tiny chest, but he could not seem to eat.

Feeds were like rounds in a boxing match, jousts that left us both emotionally and physically drained. P watched helplessly, his anxiety intensifying my own until I retreated to the privacy of the bedroom, where no one else could witness the brawl. Breastfeeding had never come naturally to me. It didn't matter how many times anyone told me that it was easy, cheap or instinctive; to me it was an algebra equation that I could never get right. I had diligently attended the NHS classes before the toddler was born, studied the diagrams, clasped the plastic doll to my breast repeating 'nipple to nose' asking myself how hard it could really be. But human babies were less compliant. The first time round I had battled on despite the pain, spending money on ridiculous contraptions that looked like metal cymbals and were supposed to soothe my broken skin. I admitted defeat four months in, mourned the intimacy of the ritual for a week or two and moved on. It hadn't been a big deal.

Now it was the physical manifestation of everything that I had been feeling all those months before: the shame, the fear, the panic, the grief. I could not get this baby to feed. The situation deteriorated and after a week of struggling I trudged up the hill to the doctor, bracing myself for that look GPs reserve for frazzled mothers with newborns. To my surprise, she didn't try to fob me off with gripe water and a sympathetic frown. I fed the baby right there in her office and she watched him writhe and kick, pulling away from me and arching his back. Then she referred me to the paediatric department at the hospital. I called P on the way home, relieved that we might be making progress, and decided in the meantime to set about finding a solution on my own.

I tried formula, buying bottles and teats that looked like accessories for a doll. The baby was game; he suckled eagerly, only for the spasms to begin again. Deliveries came so often that I covered the doorbell with a sign that said 'Pls knock' and communicated with delivery drivers in exaggerated whispers, so that the baby could get half an hour's uninterrupted sleep. I spent hours trawling the internet, reading desperate posts themselves written in the middle of the night. I searched for worst-case scenarios and panicked over wild theories about cot death. For every woman who declared it would soon be over there was another desperate and at her wits' end. The worst were those who preached endurance. I hated reading the words 'this too shall pass'. When? The baby was disappearing before my eyes. How many more weeks would this nightmare last?

Finally, I called the hospital to chivvy them along and an apologetic voice told me that the first high-priority appointment was in three months' time. I cried.

Christmas Day passed with a sigh. Usually we embarked on a week-long cross-country road trip, visiting the various outcrops of P's extended family as we went. The baby had provided us with the perfect opportunity to stay at home and I had grabbed it with both hands, assuring everyone that we were going to have Christmas as a family unit. P and I took turns to sleep in the morning, finally venturing out to the park just as daylight was beginning to fade. We both tried pushing the double buggy down the deserted city streets, road-testing this vast tank of a thing. It felt so ridiculously ungainly that it took three attempts to squeeze our way through the iron gates of the playground. The toddler stood, stationary on his new scooter in the dusk making a brrrmming noise while we took photographs to send to the rest of the family to show everyone that we were fine.

A few days later I noticed that the baby had started to wheeze. It was a dry, scraping noise, a gasp that sounded almost inhuman. Strangers stared at us on the bus. One day in the pharmacy a woman turned and said, 'My God is that your baby? I thought it was someone's phone.' I panicked, pushing bottles back on to the shelf in my hurry to get to the door. There wasn't enough air to fill my lungs; I couldn't breathe. I called the surgery, trying not to cry as I waited for the call back. 'If it gets worse take him to A&E,' the doctor said. I laid the baby on the floor and stared at him, certain that whatever decision I made it would be the wrong one.

If the days were hard, the nights were unrelenting. The baby would wake shortly after midnight, hungry and fed up. I put him to my breast and he howled as though it were acid, not milk, making its way down his throat. He beat his fists against my chest until finally hunger forced him to try again, desperate suckles which could not possibly be filling him up. I veered between hope and frustration, desperation and tears. At some point P would stagger out, relocating to the room we had prepared for the baby, leaving us to joust through the night alone.

I sang him songs, amusing myself with lyrics that almost rhymed, and walked around the creaking floorboards of my bedroom shushing. I put him down in his basket and watched him cry, too exhausted to cry myself. There were nights when he would eventually give in to sleep, his little body relaxing and his hot breath slowing on my neck. At other times he kept battling his invisible demons until morning. Finally, in the early hours, I would stagger into P's room and hand him over, grateful to crawl into the warm spot he left in the bed.

Sleep became a distant memory. Even when the baby was peaceful, adrenaline kept me wired and awake all night. I stared at the baby as he slept, convinced that he would stop breathing the moment I closed my eyes. I tried to distract myself by revisiting my old stomping grounds, newspaper websites and current affairs magazines in the US, where the world was beginning to wake. I found it exhausting. A rolling wave of anger and opinion, I skimmed through, blearily. These political upheavals and elections seemed trivial compared to the natural disaster taking place in my own home.

Instead I cast my mind back and forth like an old film reel, searching for something, anything, that would pass the time. Food and love were intimately connected, I realised. The more I thought about it, the more obvious it became. My mother communicated her love through cooking – chapatis with golden syrup after school, home-made pancakes from Delia Smith's trusted recipe at weekends. Even now I knew that there would be a piece of cake wrapped in tinfoil or a margarine tub filled with curry or casserole squirrelled away in her handbag, waiting to be handed over as we said goodbye. We had laughed about this, my siblings and I. 'Just half a banana,' we'd say to each other in a sing-song voice, giggling at the paucity of this, her final offer, one final effort to squeeze something else in.

Her mother had been the same. When my aunties joined her in the kitchen, to make a fish curry or Love Cake for a special occasion, it was more than a meal; it was a ritual, a reminder of shared experiences and unbreakable bonds. Now I realised that the urge to feed your child is primal, a way of expressing all the things as a parent you feel but cannot say. This failure between the baby and me was fundamental, proof that something had gone wrong while his fingers and toes were taking shape in my womb, when his tiny heart was beginning to beat. It was something biological, a malfunction that no doctor could diagnose.

Amid this chaos, I found myself thinking about the plants once more. It wasn't that I wanted to, more that they were now hard to avoid. The baby refused to be put down even for a moment. The only place he was happy was on my chest, so I strapped him to me like a chimp; the plants were in my eye-line as I paced around the house. I was grateful for their undemanding presence. I didn't need to talk to them, to cuddle or soothe or negotiate. I didn't need to rush or say anything at all. I observed them closely as I meandered my way for the hundredth time round the house. Their anaemic appearance seemed to echo my own.

None had responded very well to my efforts to heal them. The aloe, in particular, looked like it was drawing its last breath. A few of its spears were brown and rotting. I wondered if I ought to just give up and throw it away, but as I pulled open the bin I heard the clanking of the empty gripe-water bottles and smelled the dreadful aniseed stench. No, I thought, this at the very least I could do. It wasn't just a plant, it was my pride that was at stake.

I started reading snippets on my phone whenever I had a moment. The kumquat, I discovered, was native to China. The first plant had been brought to Europe in 1846 by Robert Fortune, a Scottish plant hunter working for the Royal Horticultural Society. Mine had started its life in the less exotic surroundings of a garden centre in Penge. I had brought it home, thinking it would live happily in a small pot, cheering up the place with its small orange fruit. Now I realised that this little plant needed at least six hours of sunshine a day. It also had strong views about water, preferring to be damp but not drenched. I peered up at the sky above, which was a desultory grey. There was not a lot I could do about clouds, but I could give it something to eat. I dug out a bottle of plant food from the back of a cupboard where it had sat unopened for years. I mixed it with water, took the pot outside and soaked it, imagining the thirsty gulping of roots below.

The research recharged me just enough to spur me on. It felt good to do something productive with my mind. What next? I had first encountered aloes in my early teens when my parents lived in the Caribbean. They grew wild there and my mother showed me how to snap off the fleshy leaf and rub the cool liquid inside to soothe scorched skin. Now I discovered that this ancient remedy, which the Egyptians had used as an embalming fluid for its anti-bacterial and anti-fungal properties, was classed as 'easy to grow' on most gardening websites. It wanted sandy soil and dry conditions. That sounded simple enough; in other words, it wanted to be left alone.

That weekend we set off across London to Kew Gardens. P suggested we stopped to visit his stepmother along the way. I knew immediately that this was a terrible idea. The toddler sang tunelessly in the back of the car as the panic swelled in my chest and the hours ahead began to form in my mind. We would listen to nostalgic memories of another baby in another time, brush off questions about food and sleep. We would analyse the baby's tiny features searching for clues about where he had come from and who he would be. It would involve long discussions about relatives I had never met. P would tell them we were proud, delighted. I would sit silently, trying not to kill the mood. 'We promised he'd have time to explore the playground,' I said firmly. P nodded his head.

In actual fact it was the train, not the swings, that caught the toddler's imagination; he spotted it parked by the lake near the entrance and dragged his father off for a tour of the gardens. It was a mild day, clear and crisp, the winter sun casting the grounds in a soft golden light. I found a bench tucked away from the path, took a deep breath and tried to relax, hopeful that the fresh air might fortify us both through the ordeal to come.

The baby's grumbling intensified, so I yanked and tugged the layers away from my chest and laid him on his side – nose to nipple, nipple to nose – bracing myself for what was to come. The baby latched and suckled for a few minutes. I froze, my back bent like a tree in a gale, not daring to move in case I shattered this tiny moment of harmony. Then the howling began. My stomach tightened as I felt eyes turning towards me. I pulled my jumper back over me, not bothering with the clasps on the maternity bra, loathing the vulnerability, wishing I could retreat behind a tree and hide. There was no chance he would even consider the other side, outraged at the mere suggestion. My breasts throbbed and I reached into my handbag for something to stop the milk from soaking my front. How long could we keep going like this until I stopped producing it altogether? How long could he survive with nothing inside?

Tears stung my eyes and I looked around to make sure no one was watching this shameless display of self-pity. Behind me there was a woman on a blanket, breastfeeding her baby while her husband ran around with a curly-haired toddler in a pink duffle coat. She looked as serene as a Pre-Raphaelite painting, her blonde hair loose and tiny white flowers dotting the grass around mother and child. Had I ever been that person, I wondered, that vision of maternal bliss? The thought seemed absurd. The blood-curdling shriek of a hungry newborn rang through the air. Mine, not hers, but her head flicked round instinctively to search for the sound. The baby looked up at me and howled. I tracked the meandering vein beneath his tracing-paper skin and thought for a second about putting him down on the wet grass. Instead, I tucked him back into the carrier on my chest and moved on.

Silhouetted against the horizon was a glasshouse, a whale of a building stranded on the bank of a lake. It had been ravaged by time, but there was dignity in its grandeur despite the peeling paint; it reminded me of the fire-ravaged skeleton of Notre-Dame. Through the steamed panels of the glass building I could make out monumental shapes inside, swathes of green stretching from floor to ceiling. There was a pile-up on the way in as a tourist battled with the dead weight of the enormous wrought-iron doors. They swung shut behind me, pushing me over the threshold and depositing me on top of an inscription carved into the floor: '1848 Restored 1957'.

The building was thronged with plants of every shape and size, scrambling, winding and sprawling like house guests who were too comfortable by far. There were palms that stretched to the roof like fans, vines that climbed like chain mail as they encircled their next-door neighbour's trunk. A cluster of trees were perched on the top of roots that strained out of the soil like ballerinas on tiptoes; beside them squid-like tentacles spilled over the edge of the bed. It was the smell that stopped me in my tracks, marching me back to a specific moment in time. It was the scent of the hot earth and humidity that greeted me when I got off the plane in the Caribbean. I could feel myself walking down the steps from the airplane, standing on the hot tarmac as though the island were breathing me in.

Water dripped from the ceiling and the chatter of people echoed around the room, a pale imitation of the squawks and shrieks of a rainforest, but real enough for me to close my eyes and pretend. It was a jungle of extraordinary proportions, a chaos of noise and colours and sounds. The smell of warm, damp soil, bouncing back off the steamy glass walls. It was as invigorating as coffee, the essence of life. This structure may have been built to show man's triumph over nature, but today there was no doubt that nature had won. Every surface had been colonised, peeling paintwork was covered in spongey cushions of moss while vines twisted and climbed up every column and pole. Every now and then the building began to rattle and crank as another rush of hot steam was released into the ether. I walked around in a daze, astonished that there were so many different shades of green.

Amid the foliage were flecks of colour. Flowers hovering in the air like hummingbirds, pulling me to them with their vivid crimson. I looked at the label: *Clerodendrum splendens.* I stared at the random numbers and codes, looking for clues. Only the date gave me any information at all: this plant had been here since 1969, when the Beatles played their last concert on the roof of Apple Records and Neil Armstrong landed on the moon. The baby had fallen asleep again, lulled by the warmth of the air and the familiar rhythm of my heartbeat. I looked down and saw a hint of colour in his cheeks for the first time. Perhaps the energy of the place was doing something to him as well. Certainly, it seemed to be having an effect on me. I felt a clarity and calm I hadn't for months. I felt I could breathe.

I made my way over to the cycads by the door, living fossils which predate the dinosaurs. I ran a hand over their scales and sinews and felt momentarily anchored here to this place. In the centre was *Encephalartos altensteinii*, the world's oldest pot plant, leaning towards the earth like the trunk of a prehistoric beast. This ancient tree was brought to Britain by Francis Masson, Kew's first plant hunter, who 'discovered' it in South Africa's Eastern Cape and brought it across the ocean in 1775.

I snaked my way down the corridors marked Africa, the Americas and Australasia. The Victorians who built this monument thought that they could organise the natural world, that they could study and observe it and ultimately bend it to their will. The plants, however, had ideas of their own. Some hovered near to the soil, timid and fragile; others crept quietly up their next-door neighbour's trunk, reaching for the pool of light at the top of the glass. Others eschewed the overcrowded soil altogether, happy to piggyback on the branches of a taller companion instead. There was opportunism, certainly, but it was harmonious.

Occasionally I recognised something, a flash of colour or even a scent that brought back a memory or a name. A vivid-pink hibiscus took me back to the daily walk to my nursery school in Morocco, when my sister and I would pull the stamens out and stick them on our noses. The leaves of the Swiss cheese plant were so vast that they seemed to mock the familiar motif that covered the walls of every east London coffee shop. This plant could not be domesticated; it was wild and glorious, a huge creature romping all the way up the wrought-iron staircase.

As much as I was struck by the spectacle of the place, I was also acutely aware of how much there was in here that I couldn't place. It was like being at a party and scanning the room for recognisable faces. There was little to help me, none of the descriptions you would find in a gallery or museum. I would have to figure them out myself. So I began to search out their quirks and idiosyncrasies: the smooth bark of the palm, the spikes of the cycads which resembled a reptile's scales, the stems that were marked like a zebra's stripes. They were undoubtedly there for a reason, I just didn't know why. The baby began to stir and I stepped out into the crisp air wondering where in this vast place the toddler had taken his father.

Standing outside, I looked at the mammoth trees around me; the skeletons of roses, recognisable by their thorns, looked up at me from the beds. These plants had mattered enough to be brought here, to be carried across oceans with great fanfare and at considerable expense, yet I knew nothing about them; I couldn't tell one from the other any more than the baby could. In front of me were some shaggy conifers, their bohemian branches lounging over the neatly trimmed lawn. I walked down the steps towards them, past a hedge of holly, and stood underneath the branches, running my hand up a knotted trunk as I read the label: Atlas cedar, from Morocco, I told the baby as though I were introducing him to a friend. I wanted to keep going, to tell him more, but I realised that I had nothing else to say.

Education held a religious importance in my family as it does for many migrants. My grandmother had been a maths teacher and it was this profession that had allowed her to bring the family here. She worked relentlessly. 'Mrs Abaya' she became to the English students, who couldn't navigate their way through the maze of syllables in her bewilderingly foreign name. She had tutored each of her six children and, years later, made valiant efforts to do the same with me – a frustrating experience for both of us. However hard she tried to communicate this world built on logic, to me it made no sense at all.

I was never a good student. I hated the abstract nature of schoolwork, the contrived problems I had to waste time trying to solve. Journalism was different: you learned on the job, not from fictional tales and hypothetical questions but from stories that were real, with answers you could hunt out with a Dicta-phone in your pocket and a pen in your hand.

Only now, confronted with this grandeur, did it occur to me that there was an entire universe around me that I had com-pletely ignored. Plants were at the root of my own family story as well. My grandmother was born in Ceylon, but she was of Italian and Dutch descent. Her ancestors were lured to the 'Spice Island' in the 1700s, intent on making money from the island's ready supply of cinnamon, nutmeg and cloves. How had I failed to consider before now that it was plants and their value that had motivated these epic voyages of man?

I set off again across the lawn, avoiding the paths that were teeming with people. I took my time now, inspecting the bare branches for swelling buds, noticing the spikes of citrus yellow standing up in vibrant crowns. Each flower rose from the stem like a gem. I rummaged in the hedgerow, trying to shield the baby from the barbs of the glossy, dark-green leaves, searching for some sort of label, but there was none. I walked on until eventually I reached the garden's border and re-joined the path that ran along the perimeter wall. We trudged past the pockets of people admiring the first camellias, perfect spheres of red around a golden-yellow orb, the vivid pink and red of the petals breaking through the buds like a baby's crowning head. The ground below was littered with those fallen petals, as though silk handkerchiefs had been thrown behind a funeral cortège – a whole life cycle playing out for the benefit of anyone who happened to be walking past.

I followed the path past a modern building, an art gallery made of glass, with a line of people waiting outside. Beside it was a pavilion, neat and solid, untroubled by architectural fashions or fads. It was unmistakably Victorian, with decorative brickwork almost as theatrical as that on our house, and a wrought-iron awning around the front to provide shade. Outside, two palm trees stood squat on either side like guards. A sign in gold lettering hung above the door: 'This gallery containing studies from nature painted by her in many lands was given in 1882 to these gardens by Marianne North.'

A couple walked out of the swing doors, still laughing to themselves about whatever it was they had seen inside. I waited until they had gone and pushed open the door, uncertain of what I would find there. It was a cool, dark alcove, wood-panelled, with the faintest smell of cedar. Another set of swing doors opened into the most extraordinary room I had ever seen. Every inch of wall was covered in paintings: azure blues, flashes of pink and gold, a patchwork quilt of colour, bold and unapologetic. The pieces jostled alongside one another for space like crowds in a football stadium; there was so much happening that it took my eyes a while to adjust.

It was a sensory onslaught and there was nothing to do but to stand in the middle, pirouette and absorb it. The paintings were divided into geographical regions of what had once been Britain's empire. There were the redwood forests of North America, the Bauhaus blue of a tropical sky. I could almost feel the sun warming my back through my clothing, the tickle of sweat around my hairline. They were floral paintings, but not like any I had seen before. There was nothing fragrant or sentimental about them. They were bold and dramatic, lurid and, at times, obscene. One row of paintings stood out from the rest: deep-purple tankards, with veined flesh and a lip that curled like a monstrous creature in a science-fiction film. They looked grotesque and menacing, held captive in gilt frames.

Once my brain adjusted to the intensity of the room, I started to pace around it – surveying the different landscapes as though each picture was a window through which you could see a different part of the world. Instinctively I made my way towards Ceylon, scouring the images for something I recognised. We had visited the island intermittently over the years, but I had gone back alone in my twenties to meet my last remaining ties to that country, my great-aunts and uncles, searching perhaps for some sense of how I fit in. The rickshaws and vibrant red flowers of the cotton tree reminded me of forgotten smells of cardamom, curry leaf and coconut oil. I thought I recognised the metal gates at the door of the botanical gardens in Candy. There was one painting that took pride of place: a series of vast trees with roots rising from the ground likes veins in the heat. Beneath it was a typed note: 'Avenue of Indian Rubber trees at Peradeniya, Ceylon.'

The paintings were all the work of one woman, Marianne North, a 'Victorian artist and intrepid explorer' according to the sign by the door. She had travelled to seventeen countries across five continents between 1871 and 1885, almost always on her own, painting nature as she saw it. There were 832 artworks in all, painted on canvas and card in the middle of jungle, desert or downpour, and 246 pieces of wood, samples of timber from tree species native to each place, carted back to line the lower third of the wall. By the front door was a large mahogany trunk of the sort she would have taken with her around the world, and a photograph of a woman in a black dress with an imperious expression sitting in front of an easel, with an enormous cactus leaning precariously close to her head.

The room had been laid out exactly as she wished it to be, the sign said. It was the eccentricity of the place that appealed to me, the sheer madness of the project and her triumph in having pulled it off. Another notice at the back of the gallery explained to visitors that mistakes had been made in the labelling of certain paintings and that one or two were in the wrong place – but these errors had been made by Marianne herself and the nature of her bequest meant that no one was allowed to resolve them. At some point she appeared to have run out of wall space and improvised with two school noticeboards covered in paintings, standing marooned in the middle of a room.

The overall impression was one of breathless excitement, a child telling a story so good that they couldn't bring themselves to pause. It was a tribute to a mission accomplished, I realised, as my weary brain tried to form coherent thoughts.

My phone rang. I heard the toddler's yelps of frustration before P had said a word. I'll meet you in the gift shop, I said. I turned round one last time, trying to absorb some of the strength, certainty and optimism from the room. I walked towards the gift shop a few minutes later. The doors opened and the toddler ran out, throwing his arms around my legs. 'Shall we go?' P asked, exhausted by his tour of duty, and I nodded as we turned to leave.

In the car, I pulled my phone from my pocket and searched Marianne's name. She had written a book about her adventures. I found an edition that was still in print and clicked 'buy'.

3

Germinationis: The Month of Germination

The windows of the waiting room at the doctor's surgery were sealed shut. Whatever the weather outside, in here the air was always dry and hot. There were posters on the wall reminding patients to book a winter flu jab and alerting them to the warning signs of bowel cancer. Beside me was a noticeboard for the patients' forum. 'We asked! You spoke! We listened!' it declared triumphantly. The space below it was empty, as it had been for the three years I'd been coming here.

I pulled off the baby's hat, loosened his cardigan and looked around me for something to distract him. This was the bleakest place I could think of, a theatre of chairs lined up in rows facing a blank custard-yellow wall. There were no toys, no little plastic

43

chairs or picture books. Nothing to acknowledge that it was mothers and babies who filled these rows so much of the time. For the longest stretch of my life I had barely seen a doctor. I hadn't needed to. On the rare occasions when my body had malfunctioned it had been in a minor way, something that could be resolved with a short burst of antibiotics. That changed the moment I got pregnant.

Suddenly I needed supervision, monitoring like an unreliable machine: urine tests, blood tests, cold hands checking that 'baby' was OK. Those cold hands had been a preparation, I realised now, a way of acclimatising you to what lay ahead. Infancy passes by in a series of medical appointments: jabs, weighing sessions, blood tests, growth charts. Time ticks by like Calpol dripping from a spoon. It was by pure coincidence that our house was moments from the hospital.

My parents had worried about us raising a family so close to A&E; brawls broke out daily on the street in front of the ward, the security guards ejecting the same drunks from the waiting room only for the paramedics to pick them up again hours later from the park down the road. The eternal presence of a figure in a dressing gown, smoking – a grim reminder of what lay ahead. But I loved the hospital. It was our own personal safety net waiting to catch us if we fell. The wail of sirens had become the soundtrack to our family life. I had spent nights there, rattling around the corridors of paediatric A&E just as I had once rattled around nightclubs until the sun came up, but no pill could make life more visceral or intense than it was here.

I had watched parents racing in, a limp body over their shoulder, terror on their faces. I had listened to the duty paediatrician as he questioned an eight-year-old boy about the bleeding wound on his wrist: had he ever hurt himself? Had anyone at home hurt him? Here, more than anywhere else I had been, you understood that raising a human was brutal and an ambush could take place at any time.

This hospital was the front line. In these corridors adults were the children; we were the ones who needed reassurance, the firm voice of a doctor to guide us through the night. It was a parallel universe where bodily functions acquired an almost spiritual significance. I had spent hours holding the toddler, a plastic pot in an outstretched arm, like a renaissance sculpture, hoping that I would catch a drop of wee.

Now it was I who was failing to thrive. I stared at the blank wall in front of me and felt myself shrink with shame. In the weeks since the trip to Kew the feeling of panic had intensified. I took care of the children automatically, with no real sense of what I was doing or why. I had become fixated on other mothers, watching them at softplay and in the park. How was it that they were able to be so effortless? Breastfeeding an infant in one arm, entertaining a toddler with the other. How could they laugh as though it was all just another day of joyful chaos when something unknowable, unspeakable, unstoppable was threatening to swallow us alive?

I stared and stared, convinced that eventually it would make sense again. That I'd be able to join in, to make small talk about teething and weaning, about nappy creams and nipple shields, but it was no good; I didn't know where to start. It reminded me of a story I'd been told at a breastfeeding class before the toddler was born, about a chimpanzee in a sanctuary who had not known how to feed her baby. Her keepers had watched the chimp starving until in desperation they brought in a breastfeeding woman to show the mother how it was done. The maternal instinct had deserted me; I was that chimpanzee.

The most disorientating thing about becoming a parent was not the practical upheavals but discovering a whole new category of love. There was nothing gentle about it. It was like turning on the ignition in a car only to realise it was really the cockpit of an aeroplane. That gale-force emotion tore through your life, ripping apart the plans and the certainty you'd built before.

Now, all of a sudden, that certainty had gone and the emotional demands of motherhood were beyond me for the first time.

In the months since his birth the toddler and I had formed routines that we fell into every night. I would lift him out of the bath, wrap him in a towel and hold him on my lap; he was a snail, a sausage roll, a ball of snow. 'I'M A BIG BOY!' he'd cry through the laughter. Now it had become an ordeal. He looked to me for reassurance, but I had nothing to give him. Were some women simply not meant to be mothers? The thought was too terrible to contemplate; what if you only realised when it was too late? I left the bathroom every few minutes, lay on my bed and gathered strength to go back. The innocence on his face as he splashed boats and submarines was devastating. I was sick with guilt. And I was exhausted. The tiredness was an iron shackle around my ankle, a dead weight that was always, always pulling me down.

The baby had adjusted his routine. I fed him every three hours, limbering up psychologically for the next session just as a boxer would for a fight. I came armed for the skirmish with bottles of gripe water and plastic syringes, rubber shields, dummies, anything that might get us through to the other side. He would latch for a few minutes at a time then refuse to take any more milk. I would hold him there as he screamed, jaw clenched, willing him to try again. The aniseed smell drowned out his own warm, sweet scent making the acid in my stomach rise.

The baby's weight was dropping and the GP was anxious now, but still we lingered in the 'urgent queue' to see a specialist. There were too many other babies grappling with an unfamiliar world; the hospital was overwhelmed. They apologised and told me again that if he stopped feeding completely for twenty-four hours I should bring him in. He sipped, drank just enough to stop me from sounding the alarm. But it was unsustainable. He seemed ghostly. I became convinced that he was disappearing before my eyes. I stripped back his winter layers, his white vest and his doll-sized nappy, and all that was left was skin and bone. With his stomach empty, the chance of any sleep evaporated further. Now it was the evenings when his demons descended. The screaming began moments before P walked in the door and continued solidly for the next six hours, while we took it in turns to get the toddler settled for the night. I tried everything I could think of to comfort him, but ended up bruised and demoralised when he failed to respond.

I felt my temper fraying. The sound of his misery made me irascible and on edge; it was a biological alarm telling me that all was not well. I snapped and snarled as the evenings wore on, unable to concentrate on anything or hold any one thought in my head. When the baby gave up, finally, slumped over like a drunk against his father's chest, the noise continued, boring holes into my brain like a drill. I knew a bit about postnatal depression. There had been a flyer, I was sure, at one of my midwife appointments the year before. I thought about news stories I'd seen, CCTV footage of a ghostly figure in a nightdress wandering out of a maternity ward, never to be seen again. That wasn't me. This wasn't an illness; it was a personal failing, something I had to grapple with and resolve in the safety of my own head.

Weeks earlier I had signed up for a conference for mothers who had lost their footing at work. It was supposed to be upbeat – solution-focused and full of ideas. Even then I had felt wretched putting my name down, but I'd forced myself to do it all the same. There might be an opportunity, an idea, a solution. The thought of actually going became more horrifying as the day approached. I didn't want to be motivated; I wanted to be alone, in bed underneath a duvet.

The baby made that impossible. I had no choice but to walk while he slept, so I may as well go there. The meeting was in north London. I smiled at the women around me, feeling like a child on her first day at school, and took a seat in the lecture theatre. No one else had brought their children. I couldn't see one buggy parked in the corridor or one small figure on a chair. The room was full of high-pitched chatter, the sound of women talking and laughing among themselves. I had planned the timings carefully to avoid having to feed him outdoors, but as I sat there I began to feel sick. This was a mistake, I realised too late as I patted the baby's back.

There were four panellists on the stage – three women and a man who talked about the possibilities of being self-employed. They spoke with passion about the empowerment of leaving an office, of breaking free from corporate life. Then the audience asked questions and the tempo changed slightly; now, all of a sudden, a lag kicked in. No one had chosen to leave work; they had been nudged, pushed. Flexible working had turned out to mean working twice as hard with half the recognition. They had decided they were better off on their own. As the people on the stage answered, there was a whisper of hesitation in the room. I looked around me and realised with surprise that there were faces I knew. There was an old friend from university, who worked for a record label and had a young daughter; I had assumed she was happy and managing perfectly well. The other I recognised from playgroups near my home. She was a chatty TV exec, confident and impressive – I had once watched her breastfeeding her eighteen-month-old while walking down stairs as though it were no trouble at all. Why were they here?

The room began to feel oppressive; I was trapped between clashing currents of disappointment and hope. Before I could consider it, I looked down and realised the baby was awake. He was gazing up and contemplating me solemnly with one large hazel eye. Then he opened his mouth and began to howl. The silence of the room amplified the noise coming from his tiny body, tugging me back to reality with a thud. Instinctively I rummaged in the backpack by my feet for a bottle, and just as quickly changed my mind. I wasn't going to feed him here. I wasn't even going to try. Instead I grabbed my bag, tightened the straps on the baby carrier and muttered apologies as I stumbled as quickly as possible to the door.

That night, my mind writhed hopelessly in the darkest of places. I saw a future I didn't want and a world I couldn't escape. I gasped for air, felt my heartbeat racing and, by the light of my phone, I began to write down a list of reasons to stay alive. They were scribbled missives of desperation; one said simply the boys, the boys, the boys.

The next morning I walked downstairs in a daze. P gave the toddler his toast, the baby strapped to him for a moment to give my shoulders some respite. I moved slowly around the kitchen, the noise of breakfast muffled as though my head was still wrapped in the duvet upstairs, when I noticed that the aloe on the kitchen windowsill looked different. Its arms, which had been pale and gently sagging, were full and healthy again, like a rubber glove that someone had crept up to during the night and filled with air. I stopped what I was doing and walked over to it, running my hands up and down its rough edges as I assessed the change. It was recovering, I thought, barely believing it myself. Within moments I was swept up again in the chaos of the morning routine, but I went back to inspect it when P and the toddler had left. The plant was indeed alive – happy, even. I had saved it from its dismal fate. It wasn't just the minor success that lifted me, but the idea that some sort of communication had taken place. I had always liked plants but I thought of them as decoration, just as I did a cushion, a nice lampshade or some other inanimate object.

Now I realised that they were sentient; they could tell me things, they could react and respond. The resuscitation of the aloe had been little more than guesswork – putting some new soil in its pot and tucking it snugly back in. But nevertheless it was a success. Now I considered light and angles as I walked;

where was the sunniest position, where was there a draught, where was it cold? I moved my surviving orchid to the window ledge, where it basked in the first rays of spring sun but was near enough to the kettle for there to be some residual humidity in the air. Then I matter-of-factly assessed the kumquat. By now it was essentially a twig with one green stem hanging limply from its crown like a defunct limb. I picked up my phone and Googled the words: how do I know if a plant is dead? A chirpy American man appeared on the screen, telling me to scratch the bark with some secateurs. I found a kitchen knife and made neat little nicks all the way up the trunk. The results were inconclusive, so I gave it some more water to drink.

I was aware that this was strange, that my behaviour was slightly deranged, like a zoo animal developing coping mechanisms as the horror of captivity settles in. Gardening had never interested me in the slightest. Quite the opposite, in fact. It was slow and faintly tedious, something a certain kind of person did after they had taken the Labrador out for a walk. I couldn't remember my own mother ever doing it either. She had a fondness for plastic plants, the kind that could be easily transported and usually sat on a windowsill gathering dust. Was planting something you were supposed to learn about in childhood? Like playing the recorder or riding a bike? If so, my own parents had been unusually remiss. Neither of them had ever showed any particular interest in it. I could vaguely remember a few months when my brother had become interested in growing vegetables, but only as a way of supplementing the meagre meals at school.

I had faint memories of honeysuckle growing at my paternal grandmother's house in Poole. Not the plant itself, which I was pretty sure I wouldn't be able to identify, but the sweetness of the name, which had captured my imagination at the time. My maternal grandmother almost certainly hadn't had time to grow anything at all. She settled in Basildon soon after she arrived in England. I could picture them all in the images I'd seen in faded photos: my mother and her three sisters in their pink saris, her two brothers in ill-fitting suits wearing comically large-framed glasses courtesy of the NHS. After that they had moved frequently, going wherever my grandmother had the best teaching job. Gardening required a degree of commitment; you had to stay still for long enough for the effort to pay off. I looked out at my sad little courtyard. Rain streaked the windows and left a glossy sheen on the bare walls, still puckered from the ivy that had clung on for God knows how long.

That night P came home from work and strapped the baby to his front, walking the length of the living room as he howled and I sat on the floor. P asked the usual questions, cautious in case he said the wrong thing. How much has he had today? he asked me. 'The best feed lasted about fifteen minutes,' I told him, staring at my phone so that I could avoid looking at him. I didn't mention that the horror of these battles now consumed me so much that I felt physically sick or that I routinely put a muslin over him, not to mop up milk but to stop my tears dropping on the side of his head as he tried to feed. I looked at my reflection in the glass of the courtyard – the outline was me, but all my features had gone.

I don't know how long I sat there, but at some point P stopped and put his arm round me. Something snapped. My reaction was instant; it wasn't civilised enough to be tears. It was an animal wail, a gasping release, the air rushing out of a helium balloon until every whisper has gone. 'I want to die.' I knew what I had to do when I woke up the next morning. The doctor's surgery, a twenty-minute uphill walk away, was in the process of being merged with a larger practice nearby. It was neither convenient nor was it good, and the fact that I still went there was simply because I couldn't face the administrative burden of having to move. Appointments were highly sought after and seldom granted. The only way to get one was to turn up in person and plead. I left the house early, the baby strapped to my chest, rehearsing the lines I was going to have to say as I walked up the hill. It was a medical problem like any other, I told myself over and over again until I almost believed it was true. There was already a line of people snaking down into the car park by the time I arrived: the infirm, the lonely, the worried well, their winter coats straining against the wind. We stood there in companionable silence as the doctor pulled up in her bullet-grey Audi with the number plate GP32 YME and walked daintily past us in a pair of towering high heels.

Doctors at this surgery lasted about as long as patients did, and I had never seen one more than a couple of times. This GP was new: a woman not much older than me, wearing a silk blouse under a black cashmere coat. She did not have children, I decided with a rush of relief. There was still one more barrier to cross before I made it to the sanctity of the waiting room. The women who staffed the reception were more intimidating than any nightclub bouncer; they were experienced interrogators, well versed in the art of despatching timewasters.

One by one we shuffled up to the plastic window panel and made our case to be allowed in. In front of me was an elderly man recovering from prostate surgery and a man in his twenties, who pulled out his earphones, blushed and mumbled that his testicle had swollen. It was hard to breathe in this airless vestibule; our collective vulnerability sucked the oxygen out of the place. As I neared the front of the queue, I cast around for the right words to suggest urgency without sounding alarm. 'The doctor told me to come back if I wasn't feeling well,' I said, hoping my eyes would convey a severity my words could not. 'I'm not feeling well.'

The receptionist glanced at the baby on my front and back up at me and nodded. I sat in the waiting room wishing I was there for something less humiliating – a smear test or a suspicious mole – something that could be explained by a swab and a course of antibiotics. Instead I was going to have to explain that my body was fine and that the problem was more embarrassing: the ability to mother, the most natural of instincts, had deserted me. My name flashed up on the noticeboard. I got up, gathered my things and made my way into the office beyond. I had decided to be as matter-of-fact as possible: the pregnancy had been difficult; we had already discussed medication, but I hadn't wanted to take it; I was in the queue for NHS therapy, but things were getting worse. I could feel her observing me up as I talked. I felt acutely aware of the oil-slick finish of her burgundy nail varnish, her precisely applied lip liner and tried not to imagine what I looked like in her eyes.

What did I do for a living? she asked. Did I have support at home? She was casting around for an excuse, a lifeline she could throw me, and I couldn't give her one. I knew how it looked. I wanted to tell her that she was right, that I had everything to be grateful for, but my brain had gone rogue; I couldn't explain it any more than she could. Instead I talked about the insomnia and the tears, that twice in the past week I had to call P and ask him to come home and help. That there were days when I just lay in bed and cried. The baby stirred on my chest and I fought the urge to cover his ears, or whisper apologies to him as I said these terrible things out loud. He sighed deeply as though he too had had enough. The doctor asked the question we both knew she had to: had I been having suicidal thoughts? I gave the only answer I could. The only one I knew wouldn't lead to phone calls and flashing lights. 'No,' I said, and recoiled in the silence that followed.

I felt lighter as walked back down the hill. It had been embarrassing and awkward. The vulnerability was uncomfortable, but I had done what I needed to do and the pressure eased a fraction now that I was no longer trying to pretend that everything was fine. It occurred to me for the first time that the pills might actually do something, that perhaps this was something that could be fixed. Still, I went to a different pharmacy to pick up my prescription, not able to face a conversation with the Bangladeshi man who ran the one near my house, whose grandson was the same age as the toddler and who was mastering three languages when all my son would do was grunt and point.

It was a young woman who took the fine green paper from my hand, barely glancing at my face as she inspected the label. She began to search the cabinets behind the till as though I'd asked her for a cough syrup, and I wondered how many of these prescriptions she was given every day. The pills would not work immediately, she warned.

But they did give me the excuse I needed to stop breastfeeding. I told P that I didn't want to give up, that I felt I ought to, which was a lie. I couldn't wait. The battles had been too fierce and gone on too long – the physical manifestation of all the upheaval in my head. Instead I'd made an appointment to see a paediatrician privately, wincing at the cost. 'Two weeks,' the receptionist said. I stocked up on formula and retreated into the baby's room to pass the time. This was the oldest part of the building; the floorboards had been here when the house was first built. During the renovation we'd discovered a tiny chimney place where the coachman would have sat, huddled on a winter's night. I liked to look at it as I held the baby, rocking backwards and forwards in an old armchair.

We'd forgotten about this room in the rush to furnish the rest of the house and it was still bare except for a cot, a single bed and the battered old nursing chair my sister had wanted to get rid of. It was the ugliest piece of furniture I owned, the colour of baby vomit, and I was grateful for it. The sparsity suited my mood. At one end of the room stable doors opened out over our bare courtyard. From there I could look out over the back gardens of the terraces behind us, the dusty path where the coach would have trundled up at the end of the day to be locked up for the night.

I could see my old life glistening on the horizon, the Shard glinting in the sunlight. The window at the other end of the room looked over the next-door neighbour's tree, cheerful pink blossom covering its bare arms like confetti on a winter bride. I walked between the windows with the baby strapped to me – up and down, back and forth, through the day and the night. The houses around us were family homes. These were not temporary crash pads that people moved in and out of for a few months at a time. Generations grew up here. People were born here; they climbed these trees and carved their names into garden walls. They got older and moved out, but they never really went away. It was a way of life I had only ever observed from a distance, visiting friends' houses for a weekend before I flew home to wherever my parents were at the time.

I looked out of our stable doors at the rectangular patch of paving tiles below us: our garden – smaller than the average car. It didn't seem to get any sunlight. What was I going to do with that?

I had found one position the baby was willing to sleep in and it felt like a miracle of sorts. I propped him over a pillow with his bottom in the air as though bent in prayer and patted his back until his breathing slowed, hardly daring to breathe myself. I thought the pills would make me sluggish, but they did the opposite; my brain began to dart around, turning over the impossibility of the situation again and again – work, money, the baby, the job. There were dead ends everywhere.

I picked up my phone and began to flick through social media: images of photogenic babies, beautiful interiors, all of it curated, insubstantial and paper-thin. Eventually I switched my phone off and looked at the book by my bed.

It had arrived a week earlier and lain there untouched ever since: the diaries of Marianne North, the woman whose gallery I stumbled into a few weeks earlier at Kew. The cover did not look inspiring. On the front there was a profile image, possibly a daguerreotype, of a woman in a high ruffled collar with a look of faint disapproval on her face and her hair slicked back like a duck in an oil spill. I could not imagine this woman enduring swarms of insects, scaling cliffs or striding through the swamps to reach the plants she wanted to, as the introductory paragraph claimed.

She looked like a priggish schoolmistress, the sort of woman whose work we had studied at school simply because she was the only female on the curriculum. I flipped it over and read the back of the book. Marianne North came from an aristocratic family and grew up at Rougham Hall, the family seat in Norfolk. There she was watched over by portraits of her ancestors. Her favourite was Roger North, her fourth great-grandfather, who had been Attorney General under James II and who, she felt sure, looked down as she ate her breakfast with an expression of approval.

What Marianne lacked in education she made up for in spirit. I thought about the small wooden trunk she had hauled around the globe, the strangeness of the paintings, so un-Victorian in the bright palette and exuberant depictions of the scenes she saw. But it was her writing that surprised me the most as I flicked through the early pages of her memoir. Her voice was crisp and witty; she seemed to be talking to me with an arched eyebrow and a weary sigh. I was instantly drawn to her. I couldn't help but be amused by her contempt for Victorian society and resolution to see the world.

As a younger woman she had travelled through Europe, Egypt and Syria with her father, a gentleman and the Liberal MP for Hastings, but it was after his death that her adventures really began. The book in front of me was the first volume of her recollections, her own account of what happened in those years. They had been reissued as part of a collection celebrating the work of nineteenth-century explorers who had pushed the boundaries of 'the life sciences' and whose work had been forgotten.

I knew I ought to shut my eyes and try to sleep in the few moments I could. Instead I thought back to the paintings I had seen covering every inch of the exhibition hall and decided to read on. I flicked through the chapters and picked up the story as Marianne arrived in Jamaica. She was forty years old when she stepped off the ship alone on Christmas Eve, recording her excitement with a volley of exclamation marks. Preliminary grumbles – the heat of the place made blankets unendurable – were quickly replaced by delight. The beauty of the sunset, the reddish pink of a wood pigeon's breast, were so exquisite that she gave up her dinner to enjoy them. Being entirely 'friendless' in such a radically strange place did not appear to bother her. She was enthralled by the beauty of this distant land.

She had travelled by sea, passing Cuba and arriving into Port Royal past a spit of sand and a mangrove swamp. On land every tree was a new form to her; the mountains rose up 7,000 feet, all creased and crumpled with indentations like brown paper. The mango trees were covered in pink and yellow flowers and the strange datura trees, with their long, trumpet-like flowers, bordered every stream. She was in a state of ecstasy, she wrote, and hardly knew what to paint first.

I tried to imagine how an aristocratic nineteenth-century woman would cope without any of the trappings of home, but Marianne didn't seem in the least bit troubled. She found her way to a local inn where the landlady gave up her own room and she made herself comfortable among piles of dirty clothes that were stored there. She tried a mango for the first time, declaring that no fruit is better. 'In Jamaica the best sort goes by the name of "number", the best sort having been brought over from India years ago with numbers attached and the names lost,' she wrote. She watched the Christmas Day celebrations from the street. If she missed her home or the traditions taking place there, she didn't show it. She was absorbed instead by the local women parading through the streets in their finest white muslin gowns, baskets laden with flowers and fruits balanced on their heads.

But she hadn't travelled this far to linger in the city. She quickly located a vast house, half hidden within the glorious foliage of the abandoned botanical gardens. She made her home on the upper floor, moving into the veranda that ran the full length of the house and gave her a view over the jungle beyond, hanging her sketches up on the opposite wall. She hired two local servants – Betsy, a former enslaved person and Stewart, who wore a military coat and saluted whenever she walked into the room – and declared that she could not have been happier. People often asked her what she ate, she observed with surprise, as though food itself was a trifle compared to the wonders in the jungle outside her door. She had dealt with the issue easily enough, buying a bunch of bananas so big that it took several men to lift it and hanging them from her ceiling like a chandelier – eating her way through them slowly until one day the string gave way and the rest had to be given to the pigs

Marianne was fearless, certainly, but there was also a restlessness to her that appealed to me. She could be curt, rude even. She made no effort to meet the island's expatriate society, despite carrying formal letters of introduction that would have guaranteed her entry into the best colonial homes. There was no such thing as a female explorer in the nineteenth century. Women who travelled usually did so dutifully, following their husbands as they were posted to corners of the empire.

Marianne did not care. She did what she wanted to do and did so unapologetically. I admired her honesty too. She had no patience for customs or sensitivities; she was there to work. She painted all day long, going out at daylight and not returning until noon. In the afternoon she painted indoors, staying out of the tropical storms that pounded down on dense spikes of St Augustine grass. From her terrace she could see bananas, rose apples with white tassel flowers, gigantic breadfruit and trumpet trees. Geraniums from the long-forgotten garden ran wild like weeds over a 200 feet high cotton tree with orchids lodged in its soft bark. Just before sunset, when the weather cleared, she ventured out again, exploring some new path, coming home in the dark.

Plants were an obsession for Marianne, but she didn't talk about them in the terms a scientist would; she rarely used Latin names or bothered much with identifying a specific subspecies. But she described them in language that was so vivid that I could conjure them out of the dark recesses of my mind. Some I actually remembered from my time there decades earlier, even though I couldn't be sure I'd really registered them at the time. I could recall the cream lobes of the frangipani flowers outside my bedroom window, the leathery skin of a soursop with its surprising milk-white flesh inside. I could picture the exact flowers she had seen climbing up the coconut palm. When Marianne talked about them there was an uncharacteristic softness in her tone, an indulgence that sounded a little bit like love. I flicked back to the beginning of the book. There was a preface written by her sister Janet, who had also edited the version I was now reading. Within this I found a line that captured that emotion precisely. 'My sister was no botanist,' she said, 'her feeling for plants in their beautiful living personality was more like that which we all have for human friends. She could never bear to see flowers uselessly gathered – their harmless lives destroyed.'

Those words stayed with me as I paced the confines of the bedroom, the baby in my arms. They stayed with me as I sterilised bottles and tried not to let my mind edge back to the cycle of worry and stress. Marianne was as much a botanist as I was a gardener; she was an uneducated, middle-aged single woman. Were it not for her wealth she would have been treated with contempt by Victorian society. But she wanted to understand the world around her, and she set out alone to do exactly that.

I was anchored to this city. I could not fly to the tropics or disappear elsewhere; I was berthed to this house and these streets, just as firmly as the baby had been tied to me. But perhaps I could find some of that same solace. Perhaps we could find some answers with this woman as our guide.

4

Frondescentiae: The Month of Coming into Leaf

The baby and I had our own routine now. We came downstairs after the noise of breakfast had faded and the house was calm again. Showers had been abandoned long ago; hot water on tired skin was a forgotten luxury since the arrival of this baby who simply refused to be put down.

I fed him first, a slightly less fraught routine now that the bottle bore the brunt of his frustration. He latched on to the rubber teat and yanked like a puppy with a toy. He gulped and pulled away again, drinking but still not nearly as much as he should be. The emotional trauma of the feeds was no longer quite so acute. Perhaps it was the tiny pill I swallowed every morning before I went into his room. The idea of medication had once felt monstrous, the ultimate admission of failure.

Now these white pills no bigger than breath mints were inconsequential. We both got dressed in whatever I found that looked clean, usually an old pair of leggings, their elastic long gone, that bunched around my legs as I walked down the stairs. For him, the same well-loved, well-worn babygrows that had been handed back and forth from one cousin to the next, the same ones I had squeezed on to his brother and which billowed around him so that he looked like a clown.

In the kitchen I made a cup of tea, put the baby in the harness which liberated my arms for the morning rounds. One by one I inspected the houseplants, poking a finger into the soil to see if it was drying out, inspecting leaves for signs of ill-health. When it came to houseplants there were, I now realised, a handful of basic rules. I had been fussing and fretting, watering far too often. What most of them wanted was considered negligence: to be fed and watered occasionally and otherwise left alone.

There were new faces on the ward now, new shapes and shades I had started to buy as I wandered around our home. An asparagus fern stood on a shelf above the television, its weightless fronds appearing to levitate in mid-air. I liked the quiet menace of the plant; the fronds looked like ostrich feathers but the stems beneath were lined with barbs as sharp as a cat's claws. If they caught your finger, blood pooled there like a raindrop on a leaf.

The philodendron was my nod to sentimentality; it sent heart-shaped leaves cascading down from a hanging basket in the kitchen like Rapunzel's hair. It was a calming way to begin the day, a long way from the days of straining to hear the news headlines on the radio as the toddler demanded another bowl of cereal.

The day really started the moment I left the house. The baby and I were both happiest outdoors. I packed in a hurry, running through the interminable list of things we needed for just a few hours outside – bottles, formula, muslins, nappies, certain that something vital would slip out again. The baby whimpered and squirmed, restless in the harness on my chest while I bent down to pick things up and put them in the rucksack. Then I looked outside to divine what the weather might bring that day. During the winter the sun missed the courtyard altogether. Now, on its higher trajectory, I could watch it making its way across the courtyard walls, inviting me to join it outside. There was still a chill in the air – a mendacious iciness reminding me that the day might at any moment change its mind. I put a woolly cardigan over the baby's all-in-one and placed the hat his grandmother had knitted for him on his head. It had earflaps and a red bobble and made him look like a cherubic garden gnome. Then I closed my coat around him and opened the door.

By now the stream of commuters trudging to the station like a column of ants had long ago dispersed. The streets were emptier, quiet save for the odd dog walker, a mother pushing her buggy, too busy for anything more than a polite smile. There were days when I knew where I was going, when I had a job in mind, a task that had to be done. More often I had no direction at all.

The total aimlessness of these days was unique to maternity leave. Aside from the odd doctor's appointment, there was no obligation to be anywhere or do anything; my only purpose was this defiant creature on my chest. We were bound together, but free to roam. On days like these I began to find myself with increasing regularity at the local supermarket. It wasn't somewhere I had ever gravitated towards before. The run-down aisles where spongey vegetables sat in pools of fridge water were a mecca for shoplifters; items were slipped into pockets and tucked up sleeves so frequently that the security guards had long ago stopped pretending they cared. But it had a well-stocked gardening section, shelves brimming with an unpretentious selection of window-box-brightening fare. Mostly they were gift-wrapped; orchids in peculiar colours – red and on one occasion a cerulean blue – sat next to mini palm trees, some of which were plonked in floral baskets and spray-painted gold. It gave me an instinctive uplift, like hearing a calypso tune played on a steel drum. I lingered by the pansies, sweet on their own but coarse and un-refined next to the velvety richness of the neighbouring violas. Seeing them just for a moment, juxtaposed against the tins of soup and Spam, made me smile. Sometimes I stopped by the herbs, running my fingers over the leaves, a disorientating rush that never failed to surprise me in the stale air conditioning of the superstore.

When I had exhausted the possibilities there I began to walk slyly past the florist, loitering like a peeping Tom. There was only one in the area, the hospital providing it with a steady foot-fall. Inside it was dark and gloomy, but outside the pots of shape and colour felt as joyful as shelves of pick'n'mix in a newsagent's window display. I could identify the basics – a rose, a carnation, a daffodil – brought here from somewhere hot, I assumed. There were others that I might have seen but had never really consid-ered before: some had the acid-green suckers an octopus used to cling to the ocean floor; others had bright-blue petals shaped like a Chinese porcelain teacup. The shop itself was small and inti-mate, a place that invited confidences and congratulations, when all I really wanted to do was disappear. My physical presence had become a nuisance to me since my mission began; it forced me to interact with the world when I wanted to glide through it unseen.

The baby's health had upended my priorities; it had allowed me to open a window and shove all those unanswerable and unsolvable questions out. My singular focus now was to get him through the next six months, and for some reason I had become convinced that it was Marianne who was going to show me how to do it. I felt reckless and excited with her voice in my head, as though I could feel her urging me on.

The garden centre was a safer destination than the shops closer to home. It was big and open enough for me to get lost between the aisles, but it was a bus ride away in the leafy village to the south where houses had expansive gardens. P and I had driven here one weekend shortly after we'd bought the house. We'd wandered around feeling painfully out of our depth, asking questions that sounded vaguely sensible and nodding at answers we didn't understand and promptly forgot anyway. We left with a clematis, a purple-flowering climber which sat in the garden for a few months and quietly died. In order to get there now I would need to get on a bus with the baby, which was something I did not want to do. The thought of being trapped in a vehicle with my screaming infant under the eyes of strangers was horrifying, but eventually the lure was too strong to resist.

After the supermarket, the garden centre was an Aladdin's cave of treasure, overflowing with specimens I could observe for as long as I liked. Around the entrance were small pots with shoots poking out of them like swords from a sheath. *Iris reticulata*, the label said, promising something big and flouncy like a lilac handkerchief tucked into the breast pocket of a dinner jacket. Inside the shop I examined the tortured, curling branches of the corkscrew hazel, a plant that seemed to belong outside the door of a witches' hut. Red and yellow flowers exploded like gunpowder sparks from the branches of the witch hazel, and at the centre of each flower was the shining metal of a bullet case. I felt weightless as I walked down the aisle, the mental equivalent of lying back in the ocean and letting your mind float.

I had no plans to talk to anyone, and if I saw a person I doubled back before they had a chance to ask if they could help. I scoured the labels for clues instead. Some showed childlike diagrams and a few words of Dutch. Others hinted at the beginning of a story. The *Magnolia grandiflora*, with big glossy leaves that reminded me of the frangipani that Marianne had seen, was named after 'Pierre Magnol', the seventeenth-century director of the

Montpellier Botanic Gardens, and its bark had anti-rheumatic properties, the label told me helpfully. My favourite care instructions were the ones that sounded unsure, as though they had been written by an anxious parent who hadn't yet figured out what worked and why: A Japanese tassel fern 'seemed to do best in dappled shade', someone had written hopefully.

In the corner I recognised the shape of something reminiscent of holidays with my parents in the South of France – a delicate young mimosa wearing a sprinkling of yellow blossom on each feather-leafed branch. The colour was unexpected: the acidic brightness of lemon sherbet, plastic buckets and summer sun. A product of Southern Europe, the label said: 'It is a grateful plant that blooms from February to May.' A grateful plant, I thought, and smiled despite myself; who could resist that? I had no idea if it was logistically possible to grow a tree in a pot, but the blossom stayed in my mind all the way home.

The purpose of these trips was not to buy anything but to absorb all the information I could. Having considered myself to be a curious person, I now realised that there was an entire world around me that I hadn't noticed at all. It wasn't just the plants about which I was clueless; I now walked around the streets nearby as though seeing them properly for the first time. Neither P nor I had ever been to this part of London before we viewed the house. I put in an offer later that day and then badgered the estate agent weekly, with the determination of a woman whose due date was fast approaching, until eventually the seller gave in. I knew nothing except that it had decent transport links and a good local pub.

That this corner of south London was steeped in history was obvious enough. The crest on the front seemed to have some letters and a date that I couldn't quite make out. We had laughed at the pretentiousness of this flourish on a building that was designed for a horse. The roads nearby were lined with Georgian terraces, presumably built for the first few members of the emergent middle class. Their front gardens were tucked behind brick walls and wrought-iron railings, offering the general public just a glance of the enviable paradise within. These houses were still redolent of grandeur – homes that were intended for City types, bankers and barristers who escaped to sprawling country houses at weekends. Beyond them was the spire of a Neo-Gothic church. It looked almost bucolic from certain angles, until you crossed the road and saw the blunt edges of the brutalist estate opposite and the neon lights of the kebab shop next door, yanking you back abruptly from the pages of a history book.

With the baby sleeping on me and Marianne in my head, I walked around in a daze. How much had the city changed, I wondered, since she lived across the river with her father in Pimlico? She had become his companion after her mother died and she was happy to live in a world that orbited around him. She was delighted with the eighty-seven steps up to the flat which kept 'mere acquaintances' at bay so that only true friends made the effort to come and see them. I doubted she had ever ventured to this side of the Thames. Across the river the city was expanding at an awesome pace, devouring the market gardens and rolling fields, rickety tenant housing springing up in their place. Marianne was shielded from the worst of the smog and the sickness by her wealth. Every day she accompanied her father on his daily walk to the House of Commons, where he would listen to the business of the day, while their retriever Jill waited for him outside. The dog 'knew all my father's haunts and ways and if he missed him anywhere would go and look for him at the Athenaeum about tea-time, where he was often to be seen sitting like a sphinx on the steps, much patted by bishops and other great people', Marianne said.

Most of the parks around me dated back to that period, when the city was expanding at a terrifying pace. Some were older than the houses that surrounded them, but while the price of bricks and mortar had soared beyond reason, these green spaces were left to manage on their own. The big park by the hospital lay adjacent to the site where the critic and essayist John Ruskin once lived. It was saved from development by local residents and opened to the public at the dawn of the twentieth century, at the same time as the hospital was established next door. They have always had a symbiotic relationship. In the First World War the park was used as an extra ward and filled with hospital beds.

Many of the green spaces that date from the post-industrial rush to develop the city were created deliberately to soothe. One of the toddler's favourite playgrounds was tucked away in a small run-down park, off a busy main road. I discovered that this was once the site of one of the city's biggest asylums, which was opened in 1846 and licensed to accommodate 362 people; the grounds stretched to twenty acres, with an area for growing fruit and vegetables which was tended by the patients. The soil there still harbours souvenirs; residents and dog walkers have unearthed a mustard spoon with the asylum initials, keys, rings and dolls.

Now I could see that its shabbiness was superficial – the space itself felt formal and polite. You entered via wrought-iron gates which opened on to tiered flower beds leading you up some small stone stairs, flanked on either side by fuchsia-pink flowers. At one end there was a terrace of houses and a brick wall ran down the other, which gave a pleasing sense of being held in – a secret garden of sorts. I could almost feel the ghost of a bandstand, women in their finest linen walking parasol in hand through the early summer sun. Behind more black railings was a well-kept lawn, and on the other side some fairground horses on springs, where I knew that a group of Eastern European men liked to sit and drink.

It never took me long to find something green; small parks and tiny residential squares hid all sorts of surprises. The most rewarding discoveries were the ones I had never noticed before,

forgotten corners of a crowded city which I found myself wanting to claim as my own. Around the back of a vast supermarket,
past a car wash and a football pitch was a pathway. If you walked
for long enough, past graffitied walls and posters warning off
trespassers, you reached a strip of metropolitan open land, empty
save for some cyclists and the occasional jogger, Lycra-clad and
absorbed in their own rhythm.

The baby and I walked there, inspecting and researching. We
didn't mind the cold, or the drizzle. The fresh air seemed to
revive us both. Clouds of cow parsley parted to reveal clumps
of nettles, a battalion of them, armed and dangerous, jostling
their way to the path. Some of these plants I knew already – the
structural globes of dandelion seeds transported me back to my
childhood in Morocco and the joy of blowing the seed heads
with a single breath. Plants were just as effective at triggering
memory as sound or smell. In French, the language I spoke when
I lived there, this flower was called *pissenlit* – to wet the bed –
and I remembered how the illicit thrill of the words added to the
joy. There must be a reason for this, I realised suddenly; why had
I never thought to ask? I looked it up online and discovered that
it was a reference to the diuretic effect of the plant. The English
name dandelion also came from the French: *dents de lion*, because
the jagged edges of the leaves resemble a lion's teeth.

The mood here was one of giddy excitement, a bacchanalian
ball tucked away from the city's streets where plants were rowdy
and unkempt. I admired the bedlam; a hawthorn tree was caught
in the moment, arms held high, trunk decked out in a skirt of
ivy. The enjoyment I got from these excursions was all the more
intense because I knew they would end too soon. At any moment
the baby could begin to stir and mutter against my chest, his
rumblings getting stronger and more insistent until I knew that
no gait, however steady, would rock him back to sleep again.

He was always furious when he woke. His little face crumpled in rage as he howled with abandon. He was tyrannical,

imperious and entirely beyond my control. He impressed me even as I wished I knew how to make him stop. A moment later, the serenity shattered, I was out of control and out of my depth all over again. I would hurry home with the same sickening panic I felt when rushing for a plane I knew was about to close its doors.

We had a diagnosis at last. It wasn't me the baby couldn't tolerate, it was milk. The only liquid I could give him sent his stomach acid shooting up his oesophagus, burning him from the inside. I had to hold him upright as much as possible to administer solutions through a tiny plastic syringe. There was a cure, the paediatrician assured me, but figuring it out would take some time. I lugged home a bag full of hypoallergenic milk from the pharmacy and set about trying to find the right combination of liquids to numb the fire inside my baby. The kitchen filled with bottles of medicine. I mixed and measured, applied droplets of water and stirred until tiny pills dissolved. The traces of powder on the counter tops suggested sleepless nights of a different sort, so far from my reality that it felt like another universe. I watched the baby intently, trying to navigate the expressions on his face – following the smiles and frowns – like contours on a map. But it was no good; I couldn't read him at all.

My mother once told me that she knew when her babies were crying, even when we were out of hearing range on the other side of the house; a mother's intuition was the theory, I suppose. I had loved it at the time, this idea that my mother had a superpower when it came to us. Now I wondered why we let ourselves believe that motherhood was instinctive and intuitive, when all that it did was to set us up for a fall. Marianne seemed to be very content with her childless state. She considered marriage to be a 'terrible experiment' and said she 'preferred vegetables' to the thought of being tied to any man. I did not blame her. Marriage was the only option for women in the nineteenth century and it meant handing over financial control. Marianne was in a rare position. She had money and connections, the chance to live her life as she wished to, and she took it. I wondered if I would have had the courage to make the same choice.

Just as I began to know the parks, so too did I recognise other people who walked within them: the man in a salwar kameez who came into the park from the hospital, pushing his young son in a wheelchair; the woman who took her mother out, supporting her elbow as they wound their way through the trees; the same drunks being lifted out of the same flower beds. I did not want to talk to them, far from it, but there was a quiet comfort in their rhythms. They were kindred spirits, my fellow explorers of the mundane. It was the plants that interested me more than the people; they were the ones I was here to observe. I could see now why Marianne preferred to paint plants outdoors in their natural settings; there was so much more to observe away from the captivity of a bucket in a florist's shop.

The daffodils were out in force now, huddled together conspiratorially like teenagers at a bus stop; you never saw a solitary stem. They were happy flowers; some were gaudy, others pale and refined with fluted petals so fine they resembled taffeta bells. I downloaded an app to try to understand how to tell them apart. I tried to learn their names; *Narcissus pseudonarcissus*, I said, repeating the syllables over and over again, testing myself as I had done for Latin GCSE.

My brain was awkward and heavy, but with concentration I could feel the cogs beginning to move. The best way to remember the names was to understand the stories behind them. So I began to collect them with the passion of a Victorian hobbyist. Daffodils were brought to Britain by the Romans, who believed their sap had healing powers. Their family name – *Narcissus* – was thought to derive from the Greek myth of Narcissus, the vain youth who became so obsessed with his own reflection that he fell into the water and drowned. It was a good name, I thought, watching its head lolling downwards as though admiring the vision below. Another theory from Pliny the Elder, the Roman philosopher and naturalist, however, suggested that it was named for its intoxicating smell, from *narkao*, to be numb.

In between these, cobalt pyramids emerged from the soil – grape hyacinths or *Muscari*, derived from the Greek 'móschos' or musk for their delicate scent. The plant was native to the Middle East, but had been growing in European gardens since the 1500s and naturalised centuries ago. The colour was mesmerising, an intense lapis blue that transported me to the Mediterranean sun. Traces of pollen from *Muscari* flowers have been found in Neanderthal burial sites in Northern Iraq, deep inside the caves, beneath the human remains. Historians believe they were put there to decorate the graves.

One day, walking north towards the river, I stumbled across a Moroccan-themed courtyard in the cloisters of an almshouse built in 1821 by The Female Friendly Society to house 'poor aged women of good character'. The society was set up to care for women, operating 'by love, kindness, and absence of humbug'. The residents, many in their nineties, were affectionately known as the 'old objects'. There was a central courtyard where climbing roses were trained up the brick walls. Benches sat in the middle like pews and there was an almost ecclesiastical feeling of peace. Round the back of the building was a 'world garden', a series of courtyards intended to pay homage to other nations with varying degrees of success.

I walked through them, not sure where I was supposed to be, until I arrived at one with a mosaic floor around a central fountain. There in the centre was the same fat palm I had seen outside Marianne's gallery at Kew. On some level, I realised, I was tracing her steps in reverse. While she ventured off to see what grew in the distant corners of the empire, I was discovering the treasures that her compatriots had brought back home.

The spiky bush decked out in miniature golden stars I kept seeing in garden hedges was a forsythia, the first species of which,

Forsythia suspensa, was brought to Europe in 1833. It would have been a rarity in Marianne's day, as coveted as the latest iPhone is today. It was 'discovered' in a Japanese garden by the botanist and surgeon Carl Peter Thunberg, and the genus was named after William Forsyth, a royal gardener at Kensington and St James's Palace, who had a mane of distinguished white hair like the man on the packet of porridge oats. The flowers looked impossibly frail, opening on bare stems, when little else was in bloom. But they were resilient foot soldiers who marched ahead of the leaves, able to withstand late frost and snow.

Was my city more colourful than Marianne's had been? Perhaps that explained the excitement I had seen in her depictions of the alien species on the gallery walls. Plants were an obsession for the Victorians, as the craze for all things exotic grew in the era of colonial rule. The terms 'orchidelirium' and 'pteridomania' were coined to describe the obsessive collecting of orchids and ferns. The first hobby-gardening books were published and amateurs kept nature diaries. Technological advances like the Wardian case, a hermetically sealed miniature greenhouse, allowed plants to survive long boat journeys and protected delicate ferns from city smog. Botany and travel combined as amateur collectors started to bring new specimens home. The euphorbia in the park, with bracts of bracing acid-green flowers, was known as 'Mrs Robb's bonnet', named after the Victorian lady traveller who found it in Turkey and carried it back to Haslemere inside her hat box.

I wasn't sure what it was about these stories that appealed to me, but somehow my brain absorbed them when it would tolerate nothing else. They were as easily digestible as the fairy tales the toddler demanded at bedtime. The fragments of time I had to spare when I wasn't walking, feeding or cleaning were now entirely consumed by Marianne. I carried her book with me everywhere, in the baby's nappy bag, in the pocket of my raincoat, in case I had five minutes to lose myself in it again. I grew accustomed to reading standing up, so I could continue as I jogged the baby up and down.

She wasn't easy company, in fact she was spiky and tough, but I could feel a cold rage beneath her civilised exterior that intrigued me and kept me reading on. By the time she was travelling, the early stages of women's suffrage were already under way. Between 1870 and 1880 meetings were set up all over Britain, with speakers like Millicent Fawcett urging women to demand equality from men. Marianne never mentions this. She didn't like being a woman; I wasn't convinced that she liked being around them either. She had a distant relationship with her mother and a complicated one with her half-sister, Janet. The only woman she admired unreservedly was Lucy Austin, a family friend, a little older than she was, who used to spend holidays at Rougham leaving trails of chaos in her wake. Lucy had a pet snake which lived in the sleeve of her dress and would poke its head out at breakfast, lapping milk from her bowl with its forked tongue. She liked to arrange it in her hair at dinner parties and had taught it a number of party tricks, including scattering jewellery across the dining table so the snake uncoiled itself and set off to collect all the items on its lithe body like beads. 'Her grand eyes and deep-toned voice, her entire fearlessness and contempt for what people thought of her, charmed me,' Marianne said.

It was her father who recognised her adventurous spirit and he alone who encouraged it to grow. Frederick North was a typical Victorian gentleman; he liked travel and he liked plants. It was only when it came to his eldest daughter, 'Pop' as he called her, that he bucked convention. He didn't push her towards marriage, instead encouraging her curious mind. Whenever he lost his seat in the Commons (which he frequently did), he and Marianne would explore the countryside together, her following him on her pet donkey, Goblin – a devil who ran at low-hanging branches in an effort to knock her off.

This wild adventure ended briefly in her early teens, when 'someone told my mother that I was very uneducated (which was perfectly true)' and she was briefly despatched to a girls' school which she loathed and complained about until she was allowed to return home a few months later. In the absence of an actual classroom, Marianne learned outdoors. One summer she borrowed from her local library two volumes on British fungi written by Mrs Hussey, an amateur mycologist and a fascinating character in her own right. Hussey was far more interested in studying mushrooms than in performing her duties as a clergyman's wife and became an authority on native species. Following her lead, Marianne began to paint every variety she could find, including one she kept in a glass in her bedroom until it exploded, unleashing a revolting smell throughout the house. Research suggested it was most likely a stinkhorn mushroom, or *Phallus impudicus*, a mushroom with a comically rude shape. These fungi were considered so shocking that Victorian zealots would sweep them away from woodland paths so as not to scandalise the young women walking there.

Perhaps it was instinctive, this desire to explore the great outdoors. I certainly recognised it in the toddler's urge to dig. He could spend hours quietly shovelling for worms. Did we grow out of the ability to be absorbed by nature? Or was it civilised out of us? Marianne had almost been persuaded to go in a different direction altogether. She loved music and the women in her family seemed to want to hope that she would be content to play and sing. But to the great relief of her father, who believed that 'all music was a horrid noise', stage fright put a stop to that. Plants suited her better in any case. She was too much of an introvert to perform. Her father had built three greenhouses and filled them with his collection of orchids, temperate plants and vines and she spent hours in there, studying, observing and learning.

Botany was one of the few areas where it was possible for women to exist to some extent alongside men and her father's connections elevated Marianne from being a mere hobbyist to something else. Through him she had contact with Charles Darwin and Sir Joseph Hooker, the first director of the Royal Botanic Gardens at Kew. It was the latter who ignited Marianne's imagination. He presented her with a hanging bunch of *Amherstia nobilis* – a tree that had been 'discovered' a few years earlier in Burma. Its two-foot crimson and yellow flowers were considered to be some of the most magnificent in the world. There had been a race among the leading botanists and aristocrats of the time to be the first to get one to bloom in England. The Duke of Devonshire kept this tree by his breakfast table inside a Wardian case. But it was Marianne who was given the winning specimen; a triumph for Kew, for her it was a glimpse into another world.

I put down the book and picked up my phone, caught off guard by the urge to plant something of my own. Something substantial that would mark this moment, something I could put in the earth, that would put down roots and stand firm. I typed the word 'mimosa' into my phone and started to read everything I could. The trees were native to Africa and Australia, one of Captain Cook's prized discoveries when HMS *Endeavour* dropped anchor at Botany Bay in 1770. Educated experts informed me that the trees and shrubs in the family would grow in mild parts of England, with good drainage and full sun. An overshadowed corner of south London might not be ideal – there was only one corner of the courtyard that could provide that, and even then I wasn't sure that in deepest winter the tree would get enough light – but I felt unusually optimistic; it was worth a shot.

The next day was a Saturday. We put the boys in the car seats and drove to the garden centre I now knew very well. I spoke to the manager and surprised myself with the confidence in my voice as I asked what felt like educated questions about pot size and soil. We wedged the tree into the boot, the feathery foliage reaching all the way to the gearbox, tickling the boys and sprinkling pollen over their heads. Back at home I put the pot in position and filled it with soil, then with P's help I leveraged our first tree into the earth. Sitting in the kitchen afterwards, I watched it lolling against the old brick wall, as out of place as a girl in a ballgown swaying on a night bus. As out of place as I was.

As the weeks passed, my curiosity grew and my walks became more adventurous. I went north towards the river, where the tower blocks were taller and the wail of police sirens more frequent. The streets here had always been down-at-heel. While those with money claimed the green spaces to the south, the charcoal burners and factory workers squatted and squeezed into the hovels lining the northern reaches near the Thames. It was no more salubrious today. I walked past the estate I recognised from months before, when my bus had been pulled over at a police cordon and a mass of flashing lights. Eight boys had been stabbed in one afternoon: carnage in the quiet of the school holidays. I had felt curiously disconnected from it at the time, aware of the tragedy yet struggling to compute that it had happened streets away from my own.

Now, as I made my way past on foot, I could look around me properly at the mechanics' garages, the homeless hostels and the takeaway food stores, the intensity of life at the city's heart. I kept walking through a small park, empty save for a dog walker and a man sipping beer. A sign told me it had once been a zoological garden, second in scale only to the one at Kew, where bears and lions had entertained the crowds. Before that it was a market garden, supplying fruit to the city centre. Now it was little more than a lawn, bald in patches and hemmed in by a tangle of nettles and brambles, the odd can reflecting the light of the sun. In front of me there was a boarded-up Victorian terrace, the posters around it suggesting that a shiny new development would soon take its place. For now, its sole occupant was a fox who watched me warily as I walked past. The Shard stood in the background like a radio mast broadcasting its message of drive and ambition, the thrum of money and wealth that made the cogs of the capital turn.

On the other side of the road was a metal gate, decorated with metal-worked sculptures of bees and butterflies. The path up from the entrance was covered in vines, the dappled light falling on a sign: 'If it isn't nailed down, you can buy it', the words said. I went inside and found myself in an extraordinary space, a garden unlike any I had seen in the city. The stone pathway was bordered by dense greenery and ferns. Above me was a pergola; a plant climbing up it gave off the heady smell of spices, within which I thought I could smell the faint but unmistakable scent of chocolate. The flower beds were lush and vibrant, and apple trees not yet awoken from their winter rest were trained up a warm wall like arrows pointing at the clouds. Tucked in a corner was a bench, hand-carved out of wood, the seat placed in the centre of the palm. It was the sort of thing you would expect to find in an ashram or a hippy campsite.

In the middle of it all was a tree, so bizarre it could have come from a children's book, with thick green spikes growing up its trunk and all the way down to the tips of its branches. 'Monkey puzzle', a handwritten chalk sign said. A small, shabby building sat in the centre, a black pavilion with an old-fashioned bell on the table outside. I walked on, towards the greenhouse beyond. I slid open the door and stepped straight into the rich smell of wet earth, more intoxicating than any perfume because it was honest and pure. I examined the tiny miracles that lined the shelves: a pink and purple flower so bright it looked like a tropical bird, a tangled mass of green hanging from the ceiling like Gandalf's beard. Behind it was something extraordinary: a cup flecked with orange and cream, purple veins running down its gullet, its lips curled over hungrily, as though it was waiting to take a gulp of air. It was a miniature version of the one in

Marianne's painting I saw back at Kew – a pitcher plant, the label said. I reached up to touch the silk of the cup and then placed a finger into the water within. On the counter beside me was a flyer with all the courses available here. I put one in my handbag and went home.

5
Florescentiae: The Month of Coming into Flower

I recognised the doctor's name the moment I saw it on the poster on the way into the surgery. I remembered the silk blouse and vertiginous heels, the number plate, and braced myself for the ice-cold blast of scepticism that lay ahead. She had been nothing but helpful last time I'd been here, but there was something about that cold, hard professionalism, the familiar aura of togetherness, that made me want to disappear.

The baby was strapped to my front dozing, lulled by the fresh air and my brisk pace as I climbed up the hill. He was more conscious of the world around him now, able to stay awake in the harness for a while, his cheek pressed against my chest, watching it all with a mournful expression in his hazel eyes. Now that we had medicine, I had almost completely abandoned the gripe water and his smell was returning, fresh-baked and delicious. I felt my stomach rumble as I fought the urge to hold him to my nose and breathe him in. I parked the buggy in the front row of the waiting room and sat down in the first line of chairs as I stared at the wall ahead. The baby immediately stiffened, flinching like an army general who wanted me stand to attention straight away. He was still tyrannical; he liked me upright, preferably moving or rocking from side to side until he could slide back off to sleep again. I sighed, smiling weakly at the elderly couple behind me as I paced the room, but I was invisible to them – their eyes were fixed on him instead, the nostalgia palpable as they shared a memory of another baby, many years ago, that neither of them would ever forget.

I picked up a copy of the NHS magazine from the plastic table in front of me and flicked through the articles. Already it seemed extraordinary to me that I had done this for a living every day until a few months ago; that I had interviewed people and written down their stories; that I had argued with editors and worked through the night, wincing at the strength of the coffee I needed to keep me going in order to meet the next deadline. It wasn't a different world but a different universe to the one I occupied now. For weeks I had been tinkering with vials of medicine, painstakingly measuring out and mixing up the eight doses I needed to give the baby every night. The idea that motherhood as I was now experiencing it could coexist with work – with anything – was absurd.

Finally, my name flashed up overhead. I left the buggy, our coats and hats piled on top of it like an airport trolley, and made my way down the corridor. There was a momentary pause while the doctor tried to place us both, followed by a brisk smile and a nod of the head.

'How are you feeling?' she asked. 'OK,' I replied, wincing at the flimsiness of the pleasantries even as we said them out loud. There was an element of truth to it, though. I had been feeling better, not my normal self, but I felt solid again, no longer battling the sense that I might simply dissolve at any given time.

Her eyes rested momentarily on the baby, as though trying to decide whether she needed to coo. He looked back at her intently until her eyes returned to me.

'How is the sertraline working?'

'It's fine. At first it kept me awake, I nearly gave up, but I seem to have got used to it now and I am feeling . . . all right.'

'We can increase the dose if you want,' she suggested. 'It's often the case that you might find you need slightly more.'

I shook my head. 'This is fine for the moment.' I stopped and she looked at me expectantly. 'I found a garden which offers horticultural therapy and I've started going along,' I said, trying to sound confident and dismissive at the same time whilst simultaneously wishing that the ground would swallow me whole.

But I was aware of a new compulsion beginning to take shape, an urge just as real as the one I used to feel about lighting a cigarette after every meal. The more tired and panicked I was, the stronger the need to be outside with my hands in the soil. I opened my handbag and pulled out the piece of paper from the mass of muslins and bottles, the baby's medicine sachets that now floated freely in my pockets, bags and drawers. It was creased and crumpled. I felt the doctor's eyes on me as I attempted to straighten it back out. 'For me to continue they need a referral from a GP.' I brandished the paper in front of me: 'Would you mind?'

She looked startled for a moment, and I felt the heat rise in my cheeks. Then she took the sheet and scoured it for warning signs, asking questions as she read. 'How did you find it?', 'What do you do there?', 'Who runs it?' I told her about the quiet afternoons under the monkey puzzle tree, making it all sound inconsequential and small, when the truth was the opposite of that. Then I watched with relief as she signed on the dotted line.

The flyer had sat in my drawer for a week or two after I had stumbled across the garden that day. Eventually I took it out and read through the courses available there. There was macramé for the twenty-something creatives in the developments across the road, composting for the earth mothers, fruit- and veg-growing for those who dreamed of a self-sufficient urban life. My eyes lingered on the last course on the list: 'horticultural therapy'. What was that? I thought.

I had tried traditional therapy before. It felt like the sort of thing that responsible grown-ups did, like filling in a tax return or going to the gym. P and I had dutifully gone along when we hit stumbling blocks in the early days of our relationship and were worried that it was a sign of trouble ahead. I had enjoyed the experience about as much as childbirth. Therapy required too much talking and too little action. I hated dredging up the emotional detritus of life and then leaving it to fester until the next appointment. I loathed the enforced sobriety of the therapist's office when my all my instincts told me to brush things off, make a joke and move on. On top of which I prided myself on being good with emotions. It was a language I could navigate with relative ease. But that was before this lump had formed inside me, the nameless mass in my stomach that I didn't want to acknowledge let alone discuss.

On a functional level, things were better. I could dress in the mornings, make it through to teatime without having to retreat to my room to cry. The black horror of those lists I had made of reasons to carry on had become less frequent, the contents less desperate. I put them in the back of my bedside drawer and tried to forget that they were there. I told P things were getting better, less because I was convinced of it than because I was conscious that he too had been sucked into a nightmare and needed to hear something good. But there was still an absence I didn't know how to address. The physical act of birth happened in a moment, a push, a cut, a cry, but love was different; it faltered and surged, it took time.

We had friends over to celebrate the toddler's birthday. I blew up balloons. P baked a cake – a replica of Thomas the Tank Engine, intricate and perfect down to the smallest detail. It took three days; at one point he attempted to drill a hole in some Oreo cookies to make wheels. I watched him working with envy – fatherhood seemed to come so easily to him. But, comparatively, the expectation on my shoulders was vast. I couldn't decide which of us had more grounds to object. There was nothing I wanted less than a house full of people asking questions, but it was my son's birthday, so I shoved the dread aside. Our friends took turns to admire the baby. Others tried to talk to me about issues in the news – politicians and scandals, the sort of thing I used to argue about every day. I tried to still the panic, the urge to open the door and run. Fortunately, children's birthday parties are the enemy of meaningful conversation. As the house filled up the volume rose until it was a jungle chorus of shrieks and wails. The chaos itself was protection; I made excuses, walking away mid-sentence claiming that I needed to stop the toddler from jumping off the stairs.

The baby's weight had plummeted again in the week before the party and finally we had made it to the front of the queue to see the paediatrician at the hospital. He was now under the hospital's supervision. I took him every few weeks, and as I peeled off his layers and placed him, tiny, bald, still furious, on the scales to be weighed, I tried to shake the feeling that it wasn't just him being monitored but me as well. I had never posed a threat to the baby, beyond my own incompetence; I was never going to do him any harm. I changed him. I washed him. I just couldn't escape the feeling that I wasn't very good at keeping him alive. The demons that had tortured him every evening, making him scream and writhe as we walked the lengths of the sitting room, had left as suddenly as they had arrived. The nights were still broken and fretful, but now I watched his lips purse like an old man's and wondered if he had given up the fight.

The next day, with the baby asleep beside me, slumped over a pillow in supplication once again, I started to type an email to the horticultural therapist asking for help. It was only after I had begun the email that I realised I had no idea what to say. The only things I had written since the baby was born were false reassurances to friends and family and those notes to myself to clear the torrent of horrors that were clouding my head. Now that I was trying to tell the truth to someone else, I was stumped. I tried to introduce myself in a way that sounded confident and bright, but the words were awkward and steeped in self-pity. I recoiled, deleted it all and then started again, stripping off the superfluous layers of politeness so that you could see the nuts and bolts:

I've been suffering with depression throughout my pregnancy and wanted to try horticultural therapy to see if it might help me through the next few months. Could you let me know a bit more about what is involved?

The reply came later that day from a woman called Bev:

I'm sorry to hear that. I currently run two groups – one mostly men who come to an allotment every week. The other is a group of women, some with physical disabilities, and some elderly women who join as well. It is a nice group, a safe one and it would be great if you came along.

It would be hard to think of an exchange more boring, but the relief was instant and completely out of proportion to what had taken place. I decided not to tell P until I knew more about what was involved. We arranged to meet for a preliminary chat the following week and I didn't want to raise my own expectations, or his, only to dash them again. Instead I tried to imagine who Bev might be as the baby and I meandered through the streets. The therapists I had come across were anxious types, human question marks, their heads forever tilted in well-intentioned empathy. They said things like, 'Why do you think that is?' and 'What do you think that means?' in a voice that suggested they already knew the answers and were waiting patiently for me to catch up.

The sun was shining when I arrived at the garden the following week. I couldn't believe how much had changed in the short time since I had last been. The delicate maroon drops on the chocolate vine had vanished, but the woody stem beside it had burst into life – layer upon layer of bright-green leaves adorned it like the skirt of a carnival queen. As I walked under a green canopy into the garden, I noticed small purple buds hung from the stem like lavender acorns – a wisteria, I realised with surprise. So the tapestry of lilac beading that draped itself down sun-kissed summer walls started like this? I hadn't noticed them before.

Bev was waiting by the door, looking nothing like I had expected. She was wearing a dark-green fleece, the garden's uniform, her blonde hair cut in a bob. She was in her fifties, I guessed. She was perky and upbeat, exactly the sort of woman who would serve a roast and then nip out with the secateurs to deadhead the roses after lunch. She swooped on the baby without a moment's hesitation, picking him up and chattering away to him looking unselfconsciously deranged. Then she led me inside to a classroom where Formica tables were shoved into corners and folders and ancient gardening books lined the walls. I sat in front of her and began, awkwardly, to explain. I started sentences and abandoned them moments later, aware that I was tying myself in knots. The pressure reminded me of the oral part of a language exam I hadn't prepared for – smiling too brightly and confidently whilst announcing to the examiner that your mother is a dog.

Bev was unfazed. She picked up the conversational baton and chatted in an uninhibited way. She had been an occupational therapist, she told me, following her husband as he moved around the world for his career. They had finally settled back here a few years ago, and she had retrained as a landscape gardener, doing the training right here at their evening class. I listened with interest.

'What does horticultural therapy actually involve?'

'It's not really therapy in the traditional sense,' she told me. 'The garden and the plants in it are the therapy, all I do is come along and supervise.'

'When does the talking happen? Do we all sit down and . . .' I fished around for the right word, trying not to grimace as I found it: 'share?'

'We don't really discuss problems in a structured way,' she said. 'But I'm always here if ever you want to chat.'

I finished my tea and nodded, conscious that a seed of excitement had found its way into my gut and settled in there. This was it – my classroom, and the key to discovering whatever it was that Marianne had found. I could learn things here, absorb information, understand what it was she had discovered a hundred years ago.

Excitement faded to dread as the first session approached. I had worn the same grey pair of leggings almost every day since the baby had arrived. They were stained and dirty, with a threadbare patch on each thigh. At some point in the past months the grimness of my appearance had started to give me a perverse thrill. I liked that my hair was greasy and tangled; my face, with its purple bags and dry patches, was a mirror of the way I felt.

Now I was going to have to feign some semblance of normality. I would have to introduce myself to strangers – to be polite and pleasant, when I had been trying for a long time to rub myself out. I had finally given in and told P that I was going to the garden, knowing that he would not let me back out. 'It's a brilliant idea,' he said as he cooked dinner over the baby's howls, delighted by the unexpected direction things had taken. 'Don't worry about it. You always try to cancel social engagements five minutes before they start.' He was right and we both knew it. I had an introvert's instinct for self-sabotage, looking forward to a party and then backing out as the moment arrived.

This time round the thought was even more horrifying. My parents were still in Australia, sending me WhatsApp images of each other with a koala. They asked about the baby and I sent them light-hearted updates, photographs of him, laying him on the floor next to a wine bottle for scale. Friends were just as easy to deflect. Technology was an effective barrier to real commu-nication, the best way of keeping absolutely everybody at bay. The only adults I had spoken to for months were doctors, P and Marianne – and she wasn't in a position to talk back.

I got ready to leave the house feeling like I was about to jump out of a plane. My plan was to push the baby in the buggy, get him to sleep, leaving me with two hours to give the therapy my best shot. I was so engrossed in packing my baby supplies (nappies, muslins, emergency medicine) and dreading the hours ahead that I failed to notice clouds gathering.

I was ten minutes from the garden when the heavens opened, a proper spring downpour, the kind that pounds the streets and sends the dust and grime of winter running down the city's drains. The scent of wet pavements was heavy and thick. I had no coat or umbrella, and I was too far to make a run for it. For a moment I just stood still in the rain, feeling my skin prickle with goosebumps as fat drops ran over my scalp. Perhaps this was divine intervention, I thought hopefully. A greater power telling me to give up and go home? Then Marianne elbowed her way into my consciousness. I pictured her as I had left her the night before – trekking through a mudslide in Brazil on a murderous mule. I knew what she would think if she could see me; I could feel her icy disdain. I snapped back to reality, pulled the plastic canopy from beneath the buggy, pulled out a muslin and wiped the baby's head before I covered him and set off again through the rain.

I was soaked from head to foot when I walked into the class-room, the baby howling dramatically from inside the pram. The drumming of the rain against the plastic cover had woken him and he was doing a fine impersonation of a car alarm. I looked at the shell-shocked faces in front of me as I burst into the room and, to my surprise, I started to laugh. It had been a long time since I had found anything funny, but the image of myself as they must be seeing me suddenly had me gasping for breath.

The women around the table composed themselves and Bev started the introductions as I eased the baby out of his cosy cocoon and began jiggling and chatting to him as I tried to restore some peace to the room. 'Rosie, meet Sarah, Sofia, Delphine and Anne,' said Bev. A woman with a mousy ponytail and spectacles glared at her with undisguised rage. I scanned the other faces and realised that I had walked into the most polite argument I had ever seen.

'I can't understand why you would send her home,' the woman in glasses said irritably.

'Because this is not the right day. Next week is the right day,' Bev replied.

'Yes, but that isn't what you said last week, Beverly.'

Now that the baby had recovered from the abrupt wake-up, I had a proper look around me. The two women sitting in front of me were staring intently at the table, apparently fascinated by their custard creams. The woman to my left had a wicked smile on her face, a look of undisguised delight. 'They're having an argument,' she observed happily.

'No we're not, Delphine,' Beverly replied. 'Anne thinks that I shouldn't have sent Helen home, and I'm explaining that I thought this was the week she was supposed to be away.' Delphine gave me a conspiratorial wink. She must have been in her eighties, but her shoulder-length raven hair and skinny frame gave her an adolescent look.

Just then I noticed that the chair next to me was not in fact empty but occupied by a tiny dog. He had a slender black body and caramel-coloured patches above each eye, like eyebrows, giving him a distinguished Napoleonic air. 'That's Bear,' Bev explained. 'He belongs to Sarah and he thinks this garden is his.' The dog sniffed in my direction. Bear was a Mexican chihuahua and he was wearing a hand-knitted green jumper. This, I would discover, was just one piece from his extensive wardrobe. He hopped down and made his way to perch on his mistress's knee. Sarah had ivory skin and a crop of short jet-black hair and she lived with her mother on the nearby estate. She spoke in a whisper so quiet that the only way to hear was to park your ear beside her mouth in a conspiratorial way.

The final member of the group was Sofia, and my first impression of her was that she was tiny, as small and delicate as a child. It wasn't until we stood to go outside that I realised she had a curved spine, she wore a stacked shoe and had a wheelchair parked nearby. The others went outside but I held back, wrestling with the utter conviction that I was in the wrong place. I was in the wrong body, even, at the wrong time. My world was fast-paced and sharp-elbowed. I argued with politicians, swore with relish and drank with the boys. I did not belong here. But nor could I think of any way to escape.

My mood lifted the moment we were in the garden. The rain had stopped and everything seemed to shine as though it had a new lick of paint. There were things growing everywhere, in the cracks between the paving stones, up the metal gates marking the perimeter wall. We walked between the rows looking properly now, with Bev stopping to explain things along the way.

There was so much growing here that I struggled to tell what foliage belonged to which plant. A tangled rose bush sprawled in one corner beside a flower bed overflowing with sage. In the middle of it all was the monkey puzzle tree. I ran my finger over the spikes, expecting them to be rubbery and soft, only to find the opposite was true; they were as sharp as barbed wire. I sucked my finger to stop the blood. Bev's tour was a multi-sensory experience. She picked a velvety leaf and handed it to me to smell: peppermint, I said with surprise. It was a pelargonium, originally from South Africa but cultivated and crossed by obsessive British collectors. These plants could be cultivated to mimic everything – they could smell of rose, of hazelnut, of Coca-Cola – like a scratch-and-sniff book brought to life. Dotted around the garden were large, squat plants as big as barrels surrounded by jutting leaves which looked less like vegetation and more like robot enemies from *Doctor Who*. They were echiums, Bev told us, native to the Canary Islands and favourites with the gardeners here, who let them self-seed at will. The leaves looked fuzzy but they were dry and rough as a cat's tongue. We followed her into the greenhouse, stopping off to inspect a *Mimosa pudica*, a distant cousin of the tree in my courtyard and recognisable from the same feathery fronds. This one was known as the sensitive plant because its leaves shut the moment they were touched.

Beauty was not the primary goal of this garden; it was a collection of curiosities. Things were left to grow where they wanted to. A large-leafed shrub had sent a runner under the soil and was now erupting in the middle of the path. No one moved it, stepping politely around it instead. I spotted bluebells growing in the borders by the street, their twee lilac petals like Victorian lampshades. But on closer inspection even this was a mirage – these were Spanish interlopers brought here in the seventeenth century and subsequently interbred with the native sort.

The more unusual a plant was, the more likely it was to be doted on. Ferns grew off the ground, held up by thick, hairy trunks; *Dicksonia antarctica*, Bev told us, a protected species native to New Zealand and Tasmania and delivered here with official paperwork to certify its 'birth'. Nearby was a tree that was stranger still; it was coarse and erratic like a vegetative incarnation of The Twits. Its name was *Pseudopanax ferox* according to a sign at its base, and it did such a convincing job of appearing to be dead that someone had scribbled 'DO NOT DIG UP' below it. Bev picked a blue-green leaf and told me to eat it; it was salty and metallic, and tasted exactly like the sea. 'Oyster leaf,' she told me, and again I was dumbfounded by the weirdness of it all.

Humans only intervened to show nature at its most miraculous. In the east corner of the garden was a tree that was doing a good job of replicating Jack's beanstalk, a *Paulownia tomentosa* or empress tree. Every year it was chopped back to its base, allowing it to perform this miraculous growth spurt, shooting up sixteen feet in twelve months before it was chopped down and started the whole thing again.

A huge clump of pampas grass had colonised a corner for itself, lounging around brushing passers-by with its long hair, a kaftan-clad hippy beckoning you in. 'Swingers used to plant this outside their houses,' Bev informed us cheerfully, 'to let others know in case they wanted to join in.' The only corner of the garden that was in any way ordered were the vegetable beds, where miniature leaves in various shades of green and deep purple sat neatly in rows, like children waiting for class to start.

We berthed in the potting shed, a cool, dark space with a pleasing smell of old soil. Nestled in among bags of compost, sieves, old boots and dried foliage, we set to work potting on seedlings – garlic plants and tomatoes that were ready to move out of their tiny incubator trays. The baby was sleeping again, strapped to my chest. The potting ledge was at the perfect height for me to work, my body free to bounce and rock whenever I thought he might be about to wake. I watched Bev's demonstration and began to ease each tiny plant out of its tray, using a wooden stick to prise it gently from the plastic case. It was delicate work and it required focus.

Hemmed in all of a sudden, my brain couldn't flutter and flap about. I had to concentrate on the task at hand and after half an hour I felt better than I had all year. But I wasn't ready to accept it yet. The way I felt in the garden was intense and exciting and it had nothing to do with the image of the sedate and sedentary pastime that was firmly lodged in my head. I interrogated myself all the way home. What was happening to me? Was it the medication? Was I imagining it? Was I just bored? 'It's Marianne's fault,' I said to the baby as I rummaged in my handbag for the front-door key.

I began to look forward to these sessions more and more as the weeks passed. Whatever happened at home – a screaming fit, an abandoned walk, a torturous night or uncontrollable tears – the anxiety began to evaporate the moment I got there. I was captivated by the changes in the garden week to week: the way the daffodils ceded the beds to the tulips, which handed the baton to the dahlias, sprinters in an eternal relay race. Perhaps it was this steady, unstoppable rhythm that had captivated Marianne, keeping her in her father's greenhouses, planting, watering and observing for so long that her face broke out in a rash. I could easily believe it. The concept of time lost all meaning in the garden. Five minutes could feel like an hour, but an hour was never enough.

'There is no such thing as a bad question,' Bev informed me that first afternoon, so I asked and asked and asked. It felt like I'd been liberated after so many weeks of solitary learning in my room. I realised now that having only read the botanical names and never heard them out loud, my pronunciation was as comical as the toddler's. A heuchera became a heu-k-era. Erysimum, not erysium. It was as elucidating as it had been to discover that Hermione was not pronounced Herm-ee-ony years after I'd stopped illicitly reading Jilly Cooper novels by torchlight. I felt like an explorer discovering pockets of brand new words after all these years.

Hopefulness underpinned everything here. The garden forced you not only to accept that there was a future, but to plan for it as well. I planted a seed for the first time, a tiny black dot like the poppy seeds I was used to seeing on a bun. I inspected it on my palm with scepticism, unable to picture the giant onion that it would become. I must have learned all of this in a classroom. Why couldn't I remember a word of it now? I wondered sheepishly. The toddler was just discovering the idea of magic. He used it to explain everything in life that did not make sense. Here I was, not far from forty, falling back on the same explanation as well.

I pushed down the soil until it felt firm beneath my fingers and sprinkled the seeds like salt, tucking them in with a layer of damp earth and anointing them with a sprinkle of water. Bev conjured up an old wheelbarrow and laid her green fleece inside it, transforming it into a cot. We took it in turns to lull the baby, pushing him around the beds, parking him finally in the shade of one of the tree ferns. There were days when he wouldn't settle, when he insisted on being held, and there was never a shortage of volunteers. It was usually Anne who triumphed. The rattiness I had seen in her that first week had vanished quickly and I never saw it again.

She had a natural empathy which the baby responded to straight away. To my surprise it worked on me as well. The idea of talking to strangers had been one of the aspects of the therapy sessions I had been looking forward to the least. But Anne's company was devoid of the judgement that marked so many interactions in the months after the baby was born. She had raised her two sons in the area, though both were now grown up. I expected her to say those things that mothers always do, like

'Enjoy it while you can, it'll be gone too soon.' Comments that made me bite my lip with frustration. Anne never said any of that. She picked up the baby and began to soften and transform. Something – the touch, the weight, the smell of his small body – seemed to unlock a corner of her head she didn't often go to; she remembered tantrums in the playground, lost rabbits, hours spent walking endlessly around parks. She enjoyed the nostalgia and so did I; for the first time since he'd been born I felt confident that one day I would feel all of this as well.

We all played second fiddle to nature; the shifting conditions told us when the next job needed to be done. The orange lights of the crocus flowers went out one by one, replaced by tulips with their lantern glow. Some were deep and generous, others fussy and petite, with frills and scalloped edges. These flowers were found growing wild in the valleys of the Tien Shan Mountains (where Kyrgyzstan meets Kazakhstan, Uzbekistan, Tajikistan and China). They were cultivated in Istanbul as early as 1055.

It was the Dutch, that great horticultural trading nation, who seized Ceylon from the Portuguese to exploit her spices. Botany was about cold hard profit long before it was about decorative bouquets. When the Dutch discovered that tulips could be grown from bulbs rather than seeds in just a year, tulip mania swept the Netherlands and the bulbs were traded instead of currency, with the rarest carrying the same value as a large and comfortable house. The leading sixteenth-century Dutch botanist Carolus Clusius was particularly fascinated by 'broken' tulips, whose petals showed a striped pattern rather than a single solid colour. The demand for these drove up the market price. Bev told us that it was actually a virus that caused the bulb to 'break'; it also made the bulbs sickly and less likely to reproduce.

I watched the bees disappearing into the snakeshead fritillaries, little alien rockets preparing to dock. These were the most extraordinary flowers. The name, I assumed, came from the chequered pattern of the petal which resembles a snake coiled and ready to strike. They hovered over the beds, their necks horizontal as though possessed by a snake charmer's song. Even the stamen looked like a serpent's tongue. Then, just as I had got to grips with that lesson, the class moved on. The fritillaries disappeared within days, to be replaced by the cheerful red and orange trumpets of nasturtiums.

It was easy to veer off into sentimentality, to find emotional resonance everywhere in the garden, but science underpinned everything here. The fritillaries were not drooping for my benefit. They did so to protect the reproductive parts of the plant from the rain. After pollination the flower straightens up so the seed pods catch the wind, throwing its head back and breathing a lungful of air. This logic only added to the garden's appeal: it was the foundation upon which the magic took place. If nature was an orchestra, then the Fibonacci code was the conductor, holding everything together with its golden ratio. The sequence, discovered in the thirteenth century, described a pattern whereby a number is equal to the sum total of the previous two. These numbers crop up everywhere; lilies and irises have three petals, buttercups and rosehips have five. Flowers in the daisy family will have either have thirty-four, fifty-five or eighty-nine petals – though each one is actually a flower, a composite made of minute miniatures. It's the same formula that explains the rotation of every seed in a sunflower head and the hexagonal segments that make up the flesh of the pineapple fruit. In nature, there are patterns everywhere.

Even more appealing was the fact that no one knew why; it was the ultimate brain twister that no one would ever crack. Pine cones have two sets of spirals, eight from one side and thirteen from the other, or five from one side and eight from the other. Leonardo da Vinci was so fascinated by these symmetries that he devised a simple formula which he believed could determine the size and shape of all trees: all the branches of a tree at every stage of its height when put together are equal to the thickness of the trunk. This still holds true today, 600 years later. In 2011 a French physicist called Christophe Eloy, who had spent years studying fluid mechanics and the air flows around solid objects, argued that trees had evolved this way so that they could hold themselves up – it is the very same principle which engineers use to keep buildings standing in a gale. Nature long ago figured it out and took man millennia to catch up.

Real-life problems felt inconsequential against the enormity of all this. The futility of our efforts made me smile. The tiny yellow flowers of a tomato plant released their pollen for only a handful of species of bee. Farmers have tried to fake it with vibrating tuning forks and electric toothbrushes, but nothing does the job as efficiently as the insects that evolved alongside the plants over thousands of years.

Marianne was born into a period of intense scientific curiosity. From the beginning of the eighteenth century collectors like the London apothecary James Petiver made use of trading ships crossing oceans to gather together specimens of insects, dried plants and seeds. His collection, which was eventually bought by Hans Sloane and formed the basis of the British Museum, was one of the largest in the world. Botanists and physicians were among the most renowned figures of the age. They were consulted by politicians and businessmen and were instrumental in the expansion of the empire. The most revered of all these men of science was Carl Linnaeus, the Swedish physician and botanist who single-handedly revolutionised the natural sciences. In 1735 he published the *Systema Naturae*, the system by which we still classify the natural world today. He used the sexual characteristics of plants (the number of stamens and pistils) to divide every living organism into genera and species, and gave them each two names to denote where they belonged within this expansive family tree.

Almost three hundred years later, I was grappling with it; I pictured Linnaeus bent over an Excel spreadsheet of epic proportions and cursed him under my breath. The unpronounceable names and irregularities made my already weary head pound. The *Euphorbia* family was a tribe of bandits, 2,000 sneaky characters as different as a cassava and a cactus, waiting to catch you out. The *Ficus* or fig family had over 850 plants, only one of which was actually a fig. Orchids, my old friends, were the worst of all, the most numerous family of plants on earth with over 27,000 different species occurring in nature and hundreds of thousands more being bred every year, almost all of them unpronounceable.

Getting to grips with it all was even more demanding than breastfeeding; I studied diagrams and filled notebooks with scrawls I couldn't recognise when I tried to read them back again. It was another of Linnaeus's big ideas that appealed to me. Years after he had won international recognition and wealth he settled at Uppsala University, teaching medicine and botany and managing a network of young botanists who travelled the world and returned with specimens for him, while he focused on increasingly far-fetched schemes back at home. One of his doomed ideas was a botanical clock, which used plants that opened and closed, depending on weather and on daylight, to indicate the time of day. Nice in theory, but no one has ever made it work. It was his *Calendarium Florae* that appealed to me. Linnaeus argued that the months of the Roman calendar should be replaced with a new system reflecting the rhythms of the natural world. The year would begin with *Regelationis*, the thawing month, followed by *Germinationis*, the budding month, and so on, until in the depths of winter we reach *Congelationis*, the month of ice. How much more bearable the dark months of winter would be if they reflected the shifting canvas outside the window.

By now the sprint of early spring had eased and an altogether more lethargic pace was taking over; I was glad to settle in with this more manageable rhythm. The big questions that had been plaguing me – whether the baby was keeping up with his weight graph, what would become of me when this maternity leave ended – mattered less now that the days were crawling past. I stopped looking at the calendar, gave up the infant development apps and watched the baby instead. He lay beneath the waving leaves of a *Fatsia japonica*, transfixed by the transition from light to shade. I watched as he ran his hands over the grass beneath him, trying to grab and lift it, only to come away with nothing. Then he did it again and again.

No one at the garden ever asked why we came, just as I never enquired what brought Sofia or Sarah here, and I was relieved not to have to tell them. But I could see how each of them changed in the garden, how they unfurled slowly and quietly like the fronds of a fern. Sofia could get out of her wheelchair and stand over the beds as she dug a hole, placed a seedling inside and firmed in the earth. The movements were awkward sometimes and Bev stood nearby, ready to give her a supporting arm. Sarah was fastidious. She worked quietly and diligently, absorbed as she moved strips of mother-in-law's tongue, rough like sandpaper, into individual pots of their own. I had never seen anyone operate with such precision and care.

The greatest transformation was in Delphine. She and Helen, who had been absent in the first class, both had dementia and were brought here by Anne, who worked for a local support group. Delphine had been a florist before her mind grew tangled and the garden was a safe haven for her, a place where things continued to make sense. Every week she arrived with a different garden implement – secateurs in one class, a dibber at the next. She would listen politely while Bev explained that day's tasks before waltzing off to do something else entirely. She planted nigella seeds in the veg beds and chopped down echiums, the head gardeners' pride and joy.

One day we were talking in the greenhouse when she spotted

a spider plant hanging from a rafter, its babies dangling from the sides like miniature pompoms. 'A *Chlorophytum comosum*,' she said instinctively as the rest of us looked on in surprise. We had the same conversation every week, she and I: 'How old is he?' she'd ask, patting the baby's downy head, and I would tell her, realising she had completely forgotten we had covered the exact same ground days before. I began to enjoy this scene we played out together; I knew what was coming and was ready to deliver my lines. For me the garden was the world in miniature, a microcosm of the universe I could study and explore. I walked around taking in the purples and yellows of wallflowers, bubbling like sugar crystal up a stick, the shaggy leaves which had put out a deep-brown flower, a monster's terrible paw, and felt myself slowly, cautiously coming back to life.

In many ways Marianne was continuing the work of Petiver and his friends. Her paintings were not intended to decorate fashionable walls; she was interested in the scientific lessons of the plants she saw in their natural habitat. This, I realised, was what gave her work such a peculiar air; they were not technical like botanical paintings, they were lessons in natural history painted in oils. The durian she paints in Singapore is about to be nibbled by a snail. The South African strelitzia is being hovered over by a native sugarbird. Nature's brutality was as interesting to her as the beauty she saw.

In Borneo she came across a strangler fig, a climbing vine which smothers the host plant to death. 'It seemed difficult to believe that those delicate velvet leaves and crimson stalks which ornament the tree so kindly at first, should start with the express intention of murdering it and taking its place,' she wrote. If there was any sentimentality in her work it was in the association between botany and her father, the man who had introduced her to this world. His death in 1869 was the catalyst for everything that came next, but she glosses over the experience of losing him in two short paragraphs.

He fell ill while they were on holiday in Gastein in the Alps and she was determined to bring him home. That last journey was so full of 'painful remembrances that I shall make the note of it as short as possible', she writes. He died at their London flat three days later, with Marianne by his side. His last words to her were: 'Come and give me a kiss Pop, I am only going to sleep.'

The perfunctory manner she deals with this in her diary only emphasised the enormous significance that moment held. It was the end of her life as she knew it; she had lost her 'own true idol' and the role of companion which had given her some status at home. More than that, she had lost her greatest supporter, and his departure, she writes, 'left me indeed alone'.

Her grief was so intense in the months after his death that she 'could not bear to talk of him or of anything else and resolved to keep out of the way of all friends and relations till I had schooled myself into that cheerfulness which makes life pleasant to those around us'. Her first stop was Switzerland, where she went 'to try to learn from the lovely world that surrounded me there how to make that work henceforth the master of my life'. But it was the chance to see the tropics that tantalised her. So she packed her paintbrushes, locked the house and left.

By now it was 1872 and I was following her travels through Brazil. Rio delighted her: 'it was the most lovely seascape in the world; even Naples and Palermo must be content to hold a second place to it in point of natural beauty'. Though Marianne was by now a seasoned traveller, she hated arriving in a new place. 'I know of nothing more trying to a shy person than that of landing for the first time amongst a strange people and language,' she wrote.

Her coping strategy was timeless and effective: 'A joke was often my most useful friend when travelling alone, helping me far more than any quantity of money (or men) could,' she remarked.

In Rio she found a kind Belgian merchant who showed her to an inn beyond the noise of the city from where she could visit the Botanic Gardens every day. She set to work immediately, ignoring Rio's expatriate society completely. She painted the gorgeous scarlet flower spikes on the bromeliads, which I imagined looking like multicoloured pineapples, and wrote passionate tributes to the creeping plants growing over with orchids and ferns. Perhaps her most dramatic painting from this period is the avenue of royal palms, half a mile long at least, with trees up to 100 feet high. 'I worked every day and all day under its shady avenues, only returning at sunset to dine and rest, far too tired to pay evening visits, and thereby disgusted some of my kind friends,' she wrote.

Instead she found a kindred spirit in the Austrian director of the gardens and his domesticated tapir, Pedro, who would snuffle treats out of his pockets as he worked all day. It wasn't just plants that interested her, but animals and insects too. She made the acquaintance of the common snail of Brazil, 'as large as a French roll and its movement were very dignified', and discovered, after keeping one as a pet in a foot-pan for a month, that it had a considerable appetite for green leaves.

She was so happy, in fact, that I was beginning to wonder if she would ever leave. But then on a trip to Corcovado Mountain she made the acquaintance of a Mr Gordon and his daughter, who invited her to visit them in the remote jungle town of Minas Geraes. Nobody but Marianne thought this trip was a good idea. It would involve crossing over 2,000 miles of muddy roads in atrocious weather. The more people told her not to try it, the more determined Marianne became.

She abandoned her tin paintbox and her gingham sketching umbrella – 'which, I may as well say here, is a perfectly useless article in the tropics' – and set off by mule, picking up a flamboyant character called Baron of Moro de la Gloria along the way. The baron had been working for the St João del Rey mining company for forty years, commanding the troop which brought the gold up to Rio every two months at least. 'He was a great character, full of talk and pantomime, either grumbling or joking incessantly, sometimes doing both at once.'

The journey was grim; they slept in barns with malnourished animals and progressed agonisingly slowly as roads disintegrated into mud. They inched forwards 'feeling for holes in a sea of pea-soup, occasionally not only finding but falling into them, a wholesome warning to those behind. The road was one constant succession of holes and traps and pies of mud, often above the mules' knees, often worn by constant traffic into ridges like a ploughed field, through which the tired quadrupeds had to wade.' Other travellers had perished, but Marianne was quite sure that the plants she saw made the whole venture worthwhile:

> Such scenery! High trees draped with bougainvillea to the very tops, bushes of the same nearer the ground reminding one of the great rhododendrons in our own shrubberies in May at home, and of much the same colour, though occasionally paler and pinker. There were orange-flowered cassia-trees whose leaves fold close together at night like the sensitive plant and scarlet erythrinas looking like gems amongst the masses of rich green.

The cecropia or trumpet-tree was always the most conspicuous one in the forest, with its huge white-lined horse-chestnut shaped leaves, young pink shoots and hollow stems, in which a lazy kind of ant easily found a ready-made house of many storeys. I devoured her descriptions as she trudged on, grumbling that the mules were going too fast for her to take it all in.

That night I pulled the duvet over me, feeling an ache in my legs and back from being outside all day. I lay listening to the baby's breath, grateful for the simple comfort of a bed and clean, fresh sheets. He woke with a howl a few hours later and dragged my mind back from the jungle where I had been walking through the rain with Marianne. I put on my slippers, picked up the bottle and prepared a medicine-filled syringe. Then I moved the rocking chair to the window and opened the curtain so that we could see the big-lobed leaves of the horse chestnut, lit by the street lights outside. They were heavy with puffs of candy-floss pink flowers just like those that Marianne had seen.

6

Grossificationis: The Month
of Fruit

'How old is he?' Delphine asked.

'He's five months.'

'Is he really!' she cried, stroking his cheek, which was as soft
and smooth as a nectarine.

It was a baking-hot day and the garden was a kaleidoscope
of green. Kermit-coloured leaves snaked up the black wood of
the potting shed like bunting. Soft, silvery foliage of a *Silene
coronaria* exploded into the pink spikes of a punk's hair. Next to
them a chorus of rock roses, with their crinkled taffeta skirts,
danced through the bed. From the middle of the madness lupins
rose up like helium balloons. Anticipation was mounting. The
garden was a room full of decorations, music playing and empty

glasses waiting to be filled. The lilac and blue flower spikes of the echiums were over sixteen feet tall, curving gently in the breeze, reckless and uninhibited, the revellers who had arrived tanked up and swaying on the doorstep. I felt light-headed too, dizzy from walking quickly in the sunshine through the city rush.

We were outside planting seeds into terracotta pots. Delphine had love-in-a-mist, Sarah had hollyhocks, I was planting thalictrum without really knowing what it was. Helen had marigolds. She shoved the seeds into the soil, sighing gently at the undemanding tedium of the task. I was glad she had been absent that first day. She was an imperious presence: ninety-four years old and with the crystal diction of a girls' school headmistress. She was tall and rake-thin, with a cloud of white hair which hovered loosely above her head and made her look like an illustration by Quentin Blake. I watched as she made her way over to the baby, asleep in his wheelbarrow, and bent over him like a willow. They stood there for a moment, divided by almost a hundred years.

'What's his name?' she asked. Bev told her. Her face contorted into an expression of pure disgust: 'Who on EARTH would call their baby that?' she demanded. And I snorted with laughter.

In the last few days the battle between the baby and me had entered a new, more challenging phase. For weeks I had tweaked doses, dissolved medication meant for adults in water and syringed tiny drops into his mouth in an effort to subdue his pain. There had been moments when I thought things were improving, weeks that passed so smoothly I began to forget how bad it had really been, but always it would come jolting back, this pain that just wouldn't let him go. Now the baby had had enough. He bucked and kicked and writhed, telling me in every way he could that he wanted it to stop. Then one morning he woke up and refused completely. That was it. He wouldn't take any milk at all.

I called 111, already sure they would tell me to take him into A&E – they did. Panicked, I rang the paediatrician, who told me what I already knew: that if I couldn't coax him to eat something somehow, we would have to take him into the hospital and the doctors would be forced to feed him through a tube. I had about a twelve-hour window to get some milk inside him. Despond-ent once again, I called P, and he came home to take over the toddler's routine. Meanwhile I did the only thing I could think of, a trick a doctor had mentioned at an appointment: I strapped him to my chest and walked until his eyelids grew heavy and his breathing slowed, then I put the bottle in. He suckled rhythmi-cally as he slept, just like the toddler did his thumb.

In the middle of this my parents returned from their travels, oblivious that our home was now a disaster zone. They swept in on a wave of excitement with photo albums and slogan T-shirts in miniature baby sizes. 'Bondi baby', one of them said, with a cartoon of an infant on a surfboard. I stared at the image, trying to think of something, anything to say. My parents were sun-kissed and happy. P and I were almost as grey as the baby, broken and battered by the first few months of our son's life. They surveyed the bottles everywhere, the toddler in his pyjamas watching TV. My mother took the baby from me confidently. 'He's very small,' she said, and immediately she began to run through her checklist of practical suggestion: babies always went through tricky phases. Perhaps he was teething, had I tried gel? Then she sat on the sofa, put her legs together with him on top of them and began to move them from side to side like an over-enthusiastic exercise instructor. This was one of her favourite tricks, the only infallible method to get a child to sleep, she had told me many, many times. The baby screamed more loudly until none of us could hear ourselves think.

Finally she gave up and let me take the wretched, red-faced infant from her. They all watched in silence as I walked the length of the sitting room until we heard his breathing slow. When his eyes were closed and his breathing steady, I picked up the bottle, put it to his mouth and he started to drink. 'I think he's ill,' my mother said finally. I looked out at the courtyard and said: 'We've got it under control.'

I left them with the toddler and made my way to the garden, so desperate to get there that I barely bothered to wipe the tears from my cheeks. The baby scared me; he knew that I hadn't wanted any of this enough, he wanted me to fail. I patted his back as I walked, willing him to stay asleep. The cherry blossom had fallen now and lined the streets outside the mechanics' garages like the palest of carpets. I weaved through the pedestrian lanes of the nearby council estate until something caught my eye. It was a small flower bed around the base of a tree, but it didn't look like the others. There were no beer cans or cigarette butts. The planting was considered and deliberate; there was vivid orange geranium, some purple violas, a sweet forget-me-not. This had not been done by the council's gardening team, I realised, as I recognised the delicate cherry scent of a red and white salvia I had seen at the garden. Someone had really thought about this.

I stopped abruptly in front of it, startled by the feeling of warmth it seemed to emit. I'd felt a similar thing in the weeks beforehand, captivated by a neighbour's garden or a collection of succulents basking on a sunny window ledge. What was that feeling? It had played on my mind as I studied the pages of plant catalogues over the baby's head. To some extent it came from me: the thrill of recognition, of knowing a plant and understanding for the first time where it belonged in Linnaeus's cursed family tree. But there was something else as well; plants were a form of expression, a way of communicating pride, care, passion for a place and for the first time those messages meant something to me.

By the time I reached the garden, I could breathe easily again. My steps were getting faster, the closer I got to those elaborate metal gates. Inside the monkey puzzle greeted me, waving spiny arms in the sky towards me with an acorn in the palm of each hand. The plants here were familiar now, each had their own personality and preference, they were as idiosyncratic as child-hood friends.

This bizarre tree had come from Chile, where it could grow on the side of volcanoes thanks to its fire-resistant bark. It was brought back to England in 1795 by Archibald Menzies, a Scottish botanist and surgeon who travelled the world collecting plants on behalf of Joseph Banks.

Banks had been the botanist on Captain Cook's pioneering voyage to the South Pacific, an expedition which made his name. He went on to supervise the king's gardens at Kew and to advise the government on various matters including the establishment of a penal colony in New South Wales. The transportation of botanical specimens began in earnest under Banks's watchful eye, always with a view to consolidating the power of the British Empire. He sent 'hunters' on voyages to South America, Africa and the Americas with instructions to bring back whatever they could find. Magnolias were brought from China, pelargoniums and proteas from the South African Cape. These plants were prize possessions, their forms and structure studied by the brightest minds. Wisteria, with its surreal beauty, waterfalls of lilac flowers hanging down in clusters like grapes, was carried here from the Far East.

I found the world of plants less intimidating now that I knew they had all been brought here. To men like Banks, nature was a treasure trove to be ransacked by whoever got their first. Of course, I knew that plantations had been a crucial part of the British Empire. I had walked between the sticks of sugar cane in the West Indies and travelled in a rickshaw through dirt paths lacing the tea plantations in Sri Lanka's hill country. But I'd never considered before the extent to which botany and commerce had driven the whole enterprise.

Sugar cane was brought from Brazil to the Caribbean, producing almost all of the sugar consumed in Western Europe in the eighteenth and nineteenth centuries. Another plant hunter,

Robert Fortune, succeeded in breaking the Chinese tea monopoly for the British East India Company by escaping the treaty ports to which Westerners were confined by disguising himself as a tea merchant. He managed to smuggle out a number of plants, keeping them alive on the journey home inside a Wardian case. These plants were introduced to India and, later, Ceylon.

Then there was rubber, another valuable story of colonial success. The sap of the Amazonian rubber tree (yet another euphorbia) had been used by indigenous cultures for centuries to make rubber balls, among other things, before the advent of motor cars led to huge demand. Spanish rubber barons built up vast fortunes cultivating the trees on expansive tracts of land (the trees are usually widely dispersed, an adaptation to protect the species from South American leaf blight). Again, the British tried and failed to break the monopoly; rubber seeds could not survive the Atlantic journey from Brazil. Finally, in 1876, Henry Wickham, an English planter, collected 70,000 of them by falsely declaring them to be 'academic specimens', a term the Brazilians used to classify dead animals and plants. He got them back to England and 2,800 of them germinated, enough to begin rubber plantations in Ceylon, British Malaya and Singapore – and end the Amazon rubber boom.

Dirty tricks like this were common. In 1787 the botanist Anthony Pantaleon Hove was despatched by Banks and the politician Evan Nepean to embed himself in the cotton industry near Gujarat. Under the guise of being a doctor he was to observe the cotton-making process and take seeds from the best varieties with a view to growing them in the British West Indies. To keep up the ruse he was instructed to write letters to his brother in Poland, where they were translated and sent on to Banks. Even my old friend the monkey puzzle was smuggled here. The seeds had been placed as decoration on top of a dessert served to Archibald Menzies while he was dining with the Viceroy of Chile. He slipped them into his pocket and grew them on board the ship back to Europe. By the time the ship berthed he had five healthy plants, the first seen in Britain.

The motivation was not always financial – not purely, anyway. Quinine, derived from the bark of the cinchona tree, was essential to guard against malaria, helping the British not just to claim new territories but to remain in them. But a shortage in production in South America, where the trees originated, led to rising prices and diminishing supplies. So in 1860 a British expedition was successfully despatched to procure cinchona seeds and plants which were established in Ceylon and Southern India.

With stakes this high, the brightest minds in Britain were coming up with ways to keep these plants alive. Banks commissioned special wooden nurseries to be built on ships, with sliding shutters and canvas covers to keep away saltwater that would kill them immediately. He issued books of instructions with notes on watering and sunlight and despatched gardeners to travel with them like night-nannies, to give them the best chance of surviving intact.

It didn't always work. For every project that succeeded, many others were catastrophic failures. On at least three occasions Banks attempted to break the Spanish monopoly of cochineal, a red dye worth more per pound than silver. Tribes in Peru and Mexico had been making it for centuries by crushing a scaly insect that lived on a variety of opuntia, or prickly pear. The Spanish had found a way to farm the insect on opuntia plantations, an extraordinarily lucrative trade. Banks tried for over a decade to break their monopoly, sending spies to South America to steal samples and masterminding efforts to replicate the process in India, but to no avail.

At times these failures were brutal. The tradesman and plant hunter John Duncan spent years securing a mudan, or tree peony, from the north of China for Banks to keep at Kew at a time when foreigners were not permitted to leave the trading area of Canton. He finally managed to get hold of a specimen, sending it off on its long journey back with careful instructions. It survived the 14,000-mile trip but died in its first winter at Kew.

Inexplicable failure was something that every gardener got used to. For weeks I obsessed over my runner beans, watching as the kidney shapes rose up the stems and from them pointed leaves emerged, like a baby dragon taking flight. Cautiously I hardened them off, leaving them in the courtyard for a few hours a day until finally they were ready to be relocated outdoors. I built a bamboo pyramid for them to climb and placed them in a large metal tub, only for the weather to turn vicious and demolish them in a storm of hail. One day the rabbit found his way into my pot of ornamental grasses and feasted like a king. Fury turned to laughter as I ran outside in my pyjamas, baby in one arm, and tried to salvage anything I could.

The more these failures happened, the less bothered I became. The window ledge in the sitting room became a nursery full of fledgling peas, parsley, lamb's lettuce and tomatoes. I felt greedy; I wanted to try to grow it all. I planted them in makeshift containers, cut-open bottles and cardboard egg boxes. I hovered over my seedlings, like the plant hunters had centuries before, misting them, making incubators out of plastic bags. There were forums full of people sharing tips and instructions, just as they did with babies. Some recommended stroking them to strengthen the stem against the wind when they moved outside. In the evenings P surveyed the chaos, finally asking: 'Do you think we've got enough?' Nope, I said absent-mindedly, huddling over my collection like a Victorian lady-hobbyist protecting her hoard.

The biggest shock was the satisfaction from the smallest sign of progress. I watched the soil anxiously until a stalk unfurled from the darkness, and savoured the triumph of knowing that something I had nurtured was growing roots and setting out on its own. I started to feel confident in my ability to take care of something – a confidence I did not know I'd lost.

There were endless parallels between caring for plants and caring for babies. Both demanded total commitment, endless care and attention and an ability to read signs so subtle you couldn't be sure that they were really there. Even the language was interchangeable. You weaned plants and grew them in nurseries. You watched their first leaves and tried to teach them independence through managed neglect. Just as my efforts were beginning to pay off in the garden, the baby was beginning to turn a corner as well. The contortions stopped as suddenly as they had started. Feeds were tolerated and a reasonable amount consumed. Perhaps it was the right balance of medicines; perhaps his tiny body had simply grown up. Whatever it was, the doctor gave me permission to introduce rusks and corn crisps, about which the baby remained deeply unconvinced – running his tongue along the edges – and looking at me with suspicion. But the improvement was undeniable. I could lay him down on a cushion on the floor without a burst of furious screaming. 'We're getting somewhere, aren't we?' I said as I brushed the remnants of compost and dried leaves out of his first tuft of hair.

Free of pain at last, a fledgling personality began to appear. He chirruped winsomely, and the laughter that had only happened in snatches before now exploded out of him until it morphed into hiccups he couldn't control. Plants also grew up in surprising ways. Some were instantly recognisable, from the moment they germinated and the baby leaves began to show. The open-handed palm of the first nasturtium leaves were miniature versions of their adult selves. Others – parsley, basil, tomatoes – emerged identical. I realised that my naming sticks were illegible and panicked as I wondered how I would know which was which.

Then I learned to relax and trust my instinct. The plants always revealed themselves gradually, with the familiar forks of a parsley leaf or the metallic tang of a tomato. The courtyard was an education on a tiny scale – a biology class and a cookery lesson all rolled into one. I planted a climbing kiwi, related to the fuzzy fruit but with small, hairless berries you could eat. I grew a Plymouth strawberry, a native plant discovered in 1627 by John Tradescant, who was collecting before Petiver was born; it had a small red berry covered in bright-green hairs and was until recently thought to be extinct. The peppery taste of nasturtium leaves was a revelation in salads. Cocktails, tea, cake – never before had I considered the many uses of mint.

Above all it was a history lesson. The more I read about Banks and his schemes, the clearer it became that the cultivation of plants and the suffering of people were inextricably linked. Slavery had existed for centuries, but the demand for raw materials to feed the social and economic revolutions taking place in Europe fuelled the trade in people in a new and horrific way. Rubber, sugar and tobacco were labour-intensive crops, and the need for a cheap workforce prompted the British to disrupt the Spanish and Portuguese slavery trade. Ships sailed from Bristol and Liverpool to West Africa, where they exchanged goods for people. The enslaved people were taken across the Atlantic to the West Indies and North America, and in the final leg of the triangular trade route the returning ships carried raw materials, sugar, cotton or rum.

The British were not the first, nor the most brutal. The rubber barons in South America were notorious for their cruelty; they captured Indians and forced them to work on the plantations. They brought workers from Africa, but still there were never enough. One baron created a stud farm, enslaving 600 Indian women whom he bred like cattle. But the relationship was even longer and more complicated than that. Petiver's collection, back at the start of the eighteenth century, would not have been possible without the slave trade. The ships were some of the most active, and the ships' surgeons – who were there to ensure the survival of the human cargo – could be trained to identify the plants he wanted and bring them back home. The plants were treated with more compassion than the people below deck, packed side by side in the cargo hold of the ship, without daylight and with barely enough food.

Later, when the plantation owners were looking for a cheap way of feeding their workforce, once again it was the botanists they turned to for help. One of Banks's most ambitious projects was the transfer of breadfruit trees from Tahiti, where they grew naturally, to the West Indies, where it was thought that they would make an economical and bountiful source of food for the enslaved workforce.

The first botanic gardens in St Vincent in the Caribbean and Calcutta in India were founded in the early nineteenth century specifically for this purpose, as well as to find new ways to disrupt the Dutch monopoly of the spice trade. Similar gardens opened in Mauritius, the Cape colony and in Peradeniya in Ceylon, where Marianne painted her rubber trees, the same place where Dutch colonisers had defeated the Kandyan royal family (killing 10,000 along the way) and where, many years later, my grandmother was born.

Kew was at the heart of it all, a botanical headquarters and sorting office for this vast machine. By the time Marianne was travelling, slavery had been outlawed in the Caribbean and South Africa and was being phased out in other parts of the British Empire, but the fascination with plants and their untapped value was still strong. There were in the region of 700 Kew-trained botanists working worldwide by the end of the nineteenth century and it was this network that enabled Marianne to travel as she did. She carried letters of introduction that opened doors with British officials posted around the empire. She wrote letters to her friends at Kew and sent dried plant specimens back.

By now it was 1876, and Marianne had travelled to Borneo as a guest of the Rani and Rajah of Sarawak. Charles of Sarawak, the third white rajah, was a nephew of James Brooke, the British soldier who had been granted land in the south-west area of Brunei as a reward for helping the Sultan to fight piracy. He had married Margaret de Windt, a handsome English lady who greeted Marianne as she stepped off the steamer. She had lost three children on a homeward voyage from drinking poisoned milk, but 'one small tyrant of eighteen months' remained.

The Rajah was shy and well liked by his people. He kept a pet mastiff which had bitten a local man, and according to their beliefs that the animal was unclean, he had agreed that it should be tried and put down in front of a public gathering, which seemed to have elevated him in Marianne's eyes. She had easy access to the lush gardens at the palace and people collected orchids and pitcher plants for her most ruthlessly. Every evening she would board a small boat with the Rani, and they would go and admire the acres of pineapples, many of them in the most exquisite pink and salmon tints, and deep-blue flowers that grew like weeds. But the women tired of one another quickly enough. The Rani was alarmed by Marianne's 'skirts kilted up to the knees and heel-less wellington boots, as though born for Borneo jungles', while Marianne was bored by her 'somewhat monotonous' constitutional walks. This was not unusual. The tedium of expatriate society was an ongoing theme of Marianne's journals; she despaired long and often of the 'croquet-badmintons' and their louche, lazy habits that seemed to blind them to the beauty of their new homes.

Wisely, Marianne decided to escape. She persuaded the Rajah to send her off out of the way to his mountain farm at Mattange. He lent her a cook, a soldier and a servant boy and packed them off in a canoe. It was here that she found what she was looking for: exquisite velvety and metallic leaves, creeping plants, foliage plants like caladiums and alpinias. She loved the drama and the discovery. She painted and explored, riding the rapids in her canoe. The most extraordinary of all were the pitcher plants, those gullets of purple flesh I had seen on the walls at Kew.

In the jungle they grew in abundance, dark and sinister, like bats hanging off trees. She festooned her balcony with the largest ones, 'over a foot long and richly covered in crimson blotches' – so big in fact that a rat could happily make a home inside. She painted and painted, and later, when the painting reached London, the great nurseryman James Veitch sent a traveller to Sarawak to hunt down its seeds. It was a new species, and Joseph Hooker named it *Nepenthes northiana*, Miss North's pitcher plant, in her honour. Not everyone would want a large, carnivorous plant named after them, but I suspect it would have pleased Marianne a great deal.

The biggest surprise, however, happened just as she was preparing to leave. Since her father's death Marianne had been a solitary figure. It wasn't just marriage that she shunned, but close friendship too. She had acquaintances and an occasional confidante, but nothing more. That changed on the steamship to Java. At first her favourite companion was the ship's captain's monkey, Jacko, who would cross his arms, put his head on one side and look at her 'as sentimentally as a young Oxford don'. Until, that was, she met the only other Englishman on board. First impressions were not favourable. They got into argument over dinner over the *Amherstia nobilis*, the plant that had cap-tivated her so long ago. It was a sacred plant of the Hindus, she informed him knowledgeably. The man contradicted her: it was not. He introduced himself as the famed Indian scholar and judge Dr Arthur Coke Burnell, famous as the co-author of the *Hobson-Jobson* dictionary of Anglo-Indian terms. Marianne was mortified and the two became firm friends.

In my mind, Marianne and the pitcher plants would always be interlinked. Now I became fascinated by plants that meant some-thing to others and the reasons why. Bev was fond of sweet peas because they had been in her wedding bouquet. Anne planted hollyhocks because growing a cottage garden in the chaos of south London gave her a subversive thrill. Delphine said there was something special about a red rose. She told me she used to work at the Savoy, then she asked me again how old the baby was.

I was a blank slate. I had arrived in this world free of pre-conceptions. To me geraniums were not a twee garden cliché but something exotic with their interconnected stems like an elaborate matchstick tower. I liked the intensity of a carnation and the lavish excess of a peony. But the plants to which I really gravitated were the happy accidents, the interlopers that crept in unannounced. I warmed to the buddleja, which shot out of every city crevice like purple fireworks. It was brought here by missionaries from China but escaped from botanic gardens and sped across the country on the railway lines, delighted to discover a plentiful supply of chalky mortar in which to grow. I loved spotting the tiny circular leaves and lilac flowers of the *Cymbalaria muralis* which crept over the city's grubby brick walls. Its common name was ivy-leaf toadflax and it had travelled from Rome, hitching a ride on a piece of marble. Eventually I set out on a quiet evening with secateurs and a freezer bag, chipped some off some bricks by the train station and transported it to my own courtyard wall.

I began to seek out these rebels, the nonconformers. It was a human compulsion to grow things that were familiar as we criss-crossed the globe. As well as bringing plants back here, Banks's plant hunters had sprinkled seeds from Kew around the world. They took oranges, lemons and apples; some were traded, others were planted in foreign ports – experiments that might come in useful for someone else who dropped anchor further down the line. The enslaved people had sometimes smuggled seeds from home. Okra, which is native to West Africa, is commonly found in the West Indies and the Americas, a souvenir from long ago.

Others travelled as stowaways, nestled within the ballast – often sand or rubble – which ships needed to stay afloat on con-voluted trade routes. Ships dropped their ballast in heaps outside busy ports in England and amateur botanists would gather to observe the curiosities that grew there.

I loved how easily these plants had slipped in and quietly taken hold, changing the landscape without a sound. *Salsola kali* from Africa was found on ballast in Avonmouth; *Amaranthus albus* from North America in Grove Quay, Bristol; *Senebiera pinnatifida* from Argentina also in Bristol; *Pisum arvense* from Portugal in Wapping Quay. Tree ferns like those of the *Dicksonia* family were a popular ballast material for ships coming from the South Pacific because they absorbed water and added weight. Most were killed off by the English winter, except those dumped around Falmouth and other mild ports. Here these hairy stumps put out roots and their descendants are still there today, waving their fronds as ships sail into the bay.

My parents, worried now, popped in with increasing frequency. Their visits were the perfect opportunity for me to escape back to the garden with the baby in tow. At first I told them I had doctor's appointments or errands, but eventually I was forced to admit that there was a group of women in a garden I liked to go and meet. They looked at me with puzzled expressions, observed the growing pile of gardening books on the surfaces, the merry chaos outside – where tomatoes jostled with rosemary and thyme for a spot in the sunshine. They noticed the plastic-bag tents over holes in the wall where I was incubating my latest finds and, still unaware of what had been happening between the baby and me, asked anxiously when I was going back to work.

I was a million miles from my former existence, as far away from real life as Marianne was when she stepped off a steamer after those long spells at sea. I understood what it was that made her keep on moving; I was happier than I had been for months.

7

Maturationis: The Month of Ripening

It was early evening, and I was sheltering in the doorway of a takeaway shop while a fight raged around me. Two groups of teenagers, hoods up and faces covered with makeshift hand-kerchief masks, chased each other across the street. Violence was common around the garden, where bored teenagers with nowhere to go kicked around looking for something to do. The lucky ones found their way inside; for many the garden was a better classroom than school had ever been. Now, though, the violence had reared up out of nowhere and I watched as these boys ran towards me, seeming to get younger the closer they got. It was the sound they made that made my heart beat faster: blood-curdling bellows of angry men. One group barricaded themselves inside a shop while the others tried to smash the glass, hurling chairs, bikes, anything they could find. I pushed myself in against the grubby glass of the door, grateful that this time I had left the baby at home.

What would I have done had he been here? I wondered. A flicker of fire leaped up in my gut – raw and ferocious. While the battle played around us, this usually bustling part of town seemed to shrink in self-defence: betting managers locked their doors, market-stall holders retreated to God knows where. A grandmother wheeled her shopping trolley away from the bus stop and backed into the entrance with me. 'Why are they doing it?' She clicked her tongue, as these children hurled threats down the road.

Less than a hundred yards away, the leaves of the banana tree swayed calmly in the summer breeze, signalling the garden's entrance: a strange oasis where people with nothing in common but their postcode came to talk. I had signed up for a course and came to the garden two evenings a week. I had been so wrapped up in my discoveries that I'd allowed myself to forget that there was anything waiting for me beyond. But a new sense of urgency had crept into my mind in recent weeks, the knowledge that this time was finite. Summer was in its element and the garden was out of control; it was a tropical jungle, a Californian forest and a wildflower meadow all rolled into one. An orgy of colour and life, sweaty and rapturous, like the scene in the glasshouse at Kew all those months ago.

I still had my afternoons with Sarah and Delphine. The baby wasn't discovering the world through playgroups and tumble, as his brother had; he was exploring the world outdoors. I laid him down on a blanket and gave him sprigs of lavender, toothed leaves from the hornbeam tree, *Carpinus betulus*, yanked out papery slips of foliage as they disappeared into his mouth. The evenings were different; they were all my own. All day I waited to hear P's key in the lock, my brain tense with excitement like a dog waiting lead in mouth by the front door. It was as though Marianne's spirit of curiosity and determination had crept from the pages and taken hold in me instead; I walked past the mechanics' garages and the takeaways feeling as focused as she had setting off into the jungle with her canvas and her oils.

When I got there I wandered between the beds, where the twining tendrils of a cup-and-saucer vine scampered over bean-poles, up table legs and rushed up towards the light. Poppies had self-seeded everywhere, some the blood-red of remembrance, others with the palest lilac frills of a ballerina's skirt. Fruit had started to form on the espaliered apples. The *Magnolia grandiflora* tree was waking up once again, producing a second display of furry cocoons as big as the baby's head. Beside it the *Musa basjoo*, the hardy banana, unfurled new leaves like a flag on a carnival float.

The other people on the course were as eccentric as any baron Marianne could rustle up. Richard was an appliance tester turned dog walker who occasionally moonlighted as a mechanic at one of the nearby garages. 'That's a marigold,' he told me confidently on day one, pointing at the thick trunk of a tree by the side of the road. By his own admission he could slaughter any houseplant, but he was not going to let this put him off. Fate had brought him to the garden, he told me. His family in Nigeria owned vast swathes of land. He had done the winter lighting at Kew Gardens, sorted out a short-circuit in the Barbican Conservatory and decided, finally, that the universe was sending him a sign.

Dom was our very own Mr Veg. A Calabrian biker who turned up in his leathers every week. He had been in London for twenty years working in care homes with people with severe learning disabilities, but his allotment was his home from home. Every day, when his shift at a local care home finished, he rushed down there to tend his tomatoes, aubergines, beans, courgettes. It wasn't work, it was relaxation, he told me. It was where he socialised as well, drinking vodka brewed by other allotment-holders from freshly grown potatoes. There was only one absolute rule for what he grew: 'If I can't eat it, I don't see the point.'

My classmates and I had nothing in common except the fact that we knew nothing at all. We didn't understand soil or tillage, couldn't tell you the difference between a spade and a shovel, between worm wee and comfrey tea. Most of us didn't even have gardens of our own. We stumbled over soil pH and forgot what colour meant acid on the litmus paper time and time again.

One evening I accidentally uprooted a banana shoot while weeding and Richard laughed so hard that he lay prostrate on the floor and shook. It was a universe where we didn't belong and the absurdity of our efforts to break in created an invisible bond. Our WhatsApp group pinged throughout the day with photographs of weeds none of us could identify – a secret society that no one else would understand. Despite my best efforts, botanical names still caused me the biggest headache of all.

'Why put all the plants into order and then name them according to no system at all?' I grumbled. 'Why do they all have ridiculous posh women's names?' By now I knew the answer: for a long time horticulture had been a rich man's pursuit. Plants were named after people they admired, often themselves. Later the cultivation of flowers took off and enthusiastic amateurs set about breeding new cultivars, hybrids that were never seen in nature, and naming them in honour of their wives; the Delphinium 'Joan Edwards', Petunia 'Belinda' and Asiatic lily, 'Patricia's Pride'. Roses were the most ridiculous; there was a Cleopatra, a Clio, a Brigitte Bardot.

The man whose challenge it was to teach us was George, a twentysomething former politics student from Derbyshire who, to his parents' distress, had jacked in a career at Westminster to teach us all about weeds. He was cheerfully unfazed by the blank faces in front of him. George knew everything about plants – names, personalities, preferred habitats. He was a reincarnation of a nineteenth-century botanist. He even looked the part, with a head of curls and a gardener's habit of wearing shorts in rain, sleet or snow. These shorts, and why he was so devoted to them, were a favourite topic of conversation among my classmates.

I grilled him periodically about his passion for plants; I wanted to understand what had sparked it, but there was nothing except for a childhood living next door to a market garden – he used to leap over the wall and help them at work. His parents thought it was a phase, perhaps they still did, but it was clear to me that this was instinctive. One of the students fell while pulling up weeds. The others rushed to help her, but I could see George checking quietly the health of the geraniums she had crushed.

The obvious place for George would have been the country-side, but I was immensely grateful that he was here instead. Most people experience London through the buildings, the nightlife, the shops. George was an expert in the city's flora. He could tell you the best window boxes to see aeoniums from the Canary Islands toughing out mild city winters outdoors. He knew exactly when to visit the butterfly exhibit at the Natural History Museum if you wanted to see the papaya tree in fruit. One day he gave us instructions to visit a nearby job centre, where he had spotted the finest specimen of a jade plant – *Crassula ovata* – that he had ever seen. 'The Department for Work and Pensions don't know what they've got there,' he said triumphantly as he drew us a map on the whiteboard.

As much as I enjoyed these evenings in the garden, there was an element of discomfort as well; maternity leave was supposed to be about the baby, yet I seemed to spend all day longing to escape. I sat in the greenhouse propagating pelargonium cuttings, chopping stems off the mother plant and trying to rationalise the guilt. To survive the past few months the baby and I had had to synchronise completely: I slept when he slept, I ate so he could. Now that he seemed to be functioning I needed to retreat again, and the garden was the obvious place to go.

The baby was unfazed by this withdrawal. The terrifying fragility of his early months had gone and in its place was an appetite at last. The doctor instructed us to start feeding him solids. It was months too early; he had no teeth and he looked at me with indignation the first time I shoved a spoon into his mouth, poking it out again with a defiant glare. I started feeding him mouthfuls of mashed banana, stewed carrot and baby rice. The more he ate, the more he enjoyed it. I thought about Marianne's descriptions of the exotic fruit she had tasted for the very first time and imagined the same awakening taking place in him. I mushed mango and avocado, *alipera* in Singhalese. Both were favourites of my mother's, fruits she picked and ate as a child and later shared with us. She had a way of preparing avocado, removing the seed and filling the hole with condensed milk, which horrified everyone I ever told but for me remained an illicit treat.

The baby swilled and swallowed, his face registering suspicion, curiosity, delight. Then I took the avocado seed, planted it in a pot and left it in the sunlight. Above all, being in the garden felt optimistic; it was an investment in a future that none of us could be sure of right now. Richard lent me his notes when I had to miss class because the baby's temperature was up. I told him some of what had happened at work: about my slide back down to the bottom of the ladder, how the last year had made me question whether I even wanted to try clamber back up again. It was tiring, joyless. It was the first time I'd really acknowledged it out loud.

No one was more surprised than I was that it was him, a man I barely knew, who I was confiding in, but Richard didn't seem shocked at all. He sent me articles about writers who became gardeners, TV presenters he thought I should look up. For him the course offered a new beginning at an age when many people thought it was too late. An opportunity to fulfil a passion and the comfort of knowing that there were others in the same boat.

Ken was a good example, a sea dog who had spent years crossing the Atlantic at the helm of wealthy people's boats; the trick, he confided to me one sunny afternoon, was to bring a supply of whisky, station yourself on the bridge and settle in for the night. You couldn't ask for more in life.

Except then he'd fallen in love and got married, and now wanted to try and make a go of it staying in one place. He'd taken a job as a postman but loathed the monotony and had always liked nature instead. His knowledge of plants was directly linked to his passion for food. His parents had owned a West Indian shop nearby. He taught me to fry okra, brew ginger beer, bake bread without kneading and make cheese on the hob. The idea that Ken was near retirement age was ludicrous – he was a whirlwind of energy; he volunteered at four parks, rescued battery chickens, went on a bee-keeping course and was relentlessly cheerful.

One day we went on a field trip to see Voldemort himself – Japanese knotweed – in a nearby garden, sliding past in single file so as not to draw attention to the intruders on the other side of the wall. We were a procession of oddities – pink-haired goths, bald bikers, note-taking grandpas. Gardening students, it turns out, make catastrophic spies. The plant itself was innocent-looking: two inches high, its delicately pointed leaves hanging from a bright-red stalk. You would never imagine that its rhizomes could travel underground, break through bricks and force apart cracks in buildings' foundations. 'How do you kill it?' asked Jack, an apprentice, with his parents' names tattooed on his arm alongside a garland of roses, their favourite flower. We learned that glyphosate, a chemical pesticide, must be injected into the stem, and that it can still take three or four years to die because the roots go down seven feet. Jack looked impressed. 'I'm going to buy one for my mum.'

Most of the young people who came here hadn't gelled with classroom life. Lee, a shaven-headed teen, had been introduced to gardening by a charity that helped kids who'd been excluded from school. He'd done all of the qualifications they could offer but he wanted to keep going and see what more he could achieve. He kept a book with him, a beginner's guide to understanding Latin names, his gardening bible, which he never let out of his sight.

Occasionally I wondered what I was doing here, a burnt-out career woman staring at a mint leaf. I was no closer to finding a plan to the problems that were festering outside the garden's gated walls; I needed to decide what I was going to do about my job, about money, about my life. But Marianne's book had pushed me to start on this journey and now that I was on it I wasn't ready to stop. It was the Victorians who set this rush in motion, when steam drove people to the cities and the population of the capital doubled in fifty years. London throbbed with a mass of humans and machinery howled through the night.

By the mid-nineteenth century, half the world's textiles were made in Britain and the output per worker was higher than that of any other country in the world. When Ruskin moved in around the corner, this area was a peaceful vantage point from which he could observe 'that great foul city of London rattling, growling, smoking, stinking – a ghastly heap of fermenting brickwork, pouring out poison at every pore'. By the time he left twenty years later the new railway line was bringing these dangers to his door. The city has not stopped growing since, nor has its pace slowed.

The more I knew about the currents that had shaped the city, the more respect I had for the outlaws that had made it their home. I could see the appeal of country houses with their orderly rows of hedging and carefully curated beds, but the city's flora was a rogue's gallery and I liked it far more.

*

Every visit to the supermarket or walk to an appointment became a field trip. Hart's-tongue ferns loved the wet shade of the tower block opposite the midwife's headquarters. Hedge bindweed wove its way in and out of the railings outside the nearby school. It was the greatest garden pest of all, so invasive that it wasn't even tolerated by George. Darwin, who spent as much time studying plants as he did animals, had observed that it only climbed counter-clockwise and made two revolutions around another plant or pole every hour and forty-two minutes. To me its white flowers looked like bells strung up to decorate the city's walls.

For each species 'discovered' in a foreign land and every crop transported, there were countless examples of nature breaking free and doing what it wanted instead. Knotweed was a prime example. *Fallopia japonica* was found growing on the side of a volcano by the German botanist Philipp von Siebold and arrived here in a shipment bound for Kew in 1854. Soon it was sold at nurseries and grown in fashionable back yards. The first plant to arrive here was a female, and with no male to cross-pollinate it was propagated instead through cuttings of the stems that grew roots and spread. Every knotweed plant in the country was descended from this one demonic female.

The plants I found growing on street corners around my home had been here for longer than I even I expected; I found records of them in *Flora Londinensis*, published by William Curtis in 1777 The humble nettle was one of the most determined, armies of them springing up in neglected corners of nearby parks, happy to tolerate sun, wind and shade. It's an extraordinarily useful plant – nutritious and anti-inflammatory. It was even used to dye soldiers' uniforms in the Second World War. And so desired by animals and insects that it would have been grazed out of existence were it not for the tiny, hollow hairs which release acid when they break. Sow thistle was the dandelion's older brother, a tougher, rangier plant with a purple tinge to its stem. It grew everywhere – on verges, the bases of lamp posts, the local skip. All it needed was a crack in the tarmac and it was off. More beautiful than any vertical garden was ivy, a ninth-century balm for sunburn and a home for the city's insects, bats and mice, so delicious to the bees that I almost regretted pulling ours down. Even the moss I'd spotted on the damp brickwork of the railway arches was something worth recognising: swan's-neck thyme-moss which sent up tiny stalks like a periscope rising from the deep. It seemed remarkable that these same plants had been here in the city for 300 years. That they had seen horses give way to cars and traffic fill the streets. These were the real London-ers, silent companions to our noise and haste, the quiet heroes growing in the shade of skyscrapers and dusty verges, filtering pollution and breathing out oxygen instead.

The garden was having an effect on my body as well as my head. Two caesarean sections in two years had left my stomach muscles ravaged and sore. The angry red gash between my hips was fading to a soft pink, but I ached more easily and tried to avoid my naked reflection when I got ready for bed at night. It felt good to be heaving and lifting after months of hobbling and fragility; pregnancy had made me feel weak. I liked the expectation that I could dig soil and uproot shrubs beside the others. I let rip around the garden with a leaf-blower feeling like a superhero and recorded myself to show the boys. One day we joined the trainees in the blistering heat of a late-summer afternoon, sorting out some beds on a nearby estate. They had been colonised by dock, an innocent in my mind until now, the soothing balm to the stinging nettle's bite. Not so, it tran-spired. The flower spikes, like rusted metal washed up by the sea, took on a sinister air with their never-ending taproots as I dug deeper and deeper down. There was something unsettling about opening up the bowels of the city and finding that there was another world down there, which other organisms had claimed as their own.

The work was tough. I felt my muscles burn and looked forward to the ache I'd feel in them the next day. We cleared away the rubbish, pulled out glass bottles, beer cans, filling up bag after bag of waste. One of my classmates called me over to the other bed – and showed me a condom packet, the prophylactic tucked neatly back inside. 'At least someone's enjoying nature,' he said, and I laughed so hard that my stomach muscles ached even more.

We perched on the edge of the wall and ate crisps and ice cream for lunch. 'Good honest work,' George said happily as he ate his Dairy Milk, and he was right. We dug up an echium that had self-seeded too close to the fence to survive there. It took five of us two hours of kicking and digging and jumping on spades to break through the dry soil. The root beneath the ground was even more astonishing than the plant above it – a vast, thick taproot that bored down, down, down. It was almost three feet long when we got to the bottom of it and it felt dense and weighty, like some sort of prehistoric bone. Jack held it up triumphantly. 'Hey, George, is it all right if I take it home?'

The people in the garden had roots as diverse as those of the plants. Nigeria, Sri Lanka, Egypt, the Caribbean – we were the human incarnations of the paintings on Marianne's wall. She had reached Ceylon and I braced myself for this chapter with a weary sigh. Her racism had festered like a boil between us since we started this adventure. I had observed the curious disregard in her references to 'natives', the icy superiority when she talked about 'negroes' and 'half-castes'.

For a while I had tried to defend her – she was, after all, a product of her time. But this felt increasingly unconvincing when in so many other ways she was not. The Abolition of Slavery Act had been passed in 1833, when Marianne was three years old. But the Abolitionist movement had opposed the trade of African people since the 1770s and public mood shifted dramatically over the course of the next sixty years. Abolitionist petitions organised in 1833 garnered the support of 1.3 million signatories. Yet Marianne showed me how, for others, attitudes had not really changed at all.

In Brazil, where slavery was still being phased out when she arrived, she observed 'little black boys' who 'looked very happy, and as if they enjoyed the process of being fatted up'. Mothers in the country had stopped caring for babies who were born free 'because they were now worth nothing'. By now I had had enough. Her wit was less witty and her company no longer fun. How was it possible to find beauty and value in the 'noble avenue of India rubber trees' at the entrance to the Peradeniya Botanical Gardens, while bemoaning the 'idle natives' whose island had been exploited by outsiders for 400 years?

At times, her views were so repugnant that I felt guilty reading them. The racism you encounter in books and on television is sanitised, tidied up and blunted down into something less vile. Now I was seeing prejudice laid out in black and white by someone I liked and admired. It was shocking. But like this you could see the inconsistencies. It was superiority wrapped up in bad science and absorbed for too long as fact.

Marianne was staying nearby at the home of her friend Julia Margaret Cameron, another unusual woman for her time. Her husband, Charles Hay Cameron, was a legal reformer who had invested in the coffee plantations there (which would soon fail across the island and be replaced by tea). But Mrs Cameron's fame eclipsed his. She had been given a camera by one of her daughters for her forty-eighth birthday, turned the chicken coop into a studio and became one of the most important photographers of the nineteenth century. While her peers were concerned with replicating reality, Cameron's images were haunting and uncomfortable, years ahead of their time.

Marianne was not a willing subject. 'She made up her mind at once that she would photograph me, and for three days she kept herself in a fever of excitement about it,' she wrote. 'She dressed me up in flowing draperies of cashmere wool, let down my hair, and made me stand with spiky cocoa-nut branches running into my head . . . and told me to look perfectly natural (with the thermometer standing at 96 degrees).' Cameron tried a different background, with no more success. 'She wasted twelve plates, and an enormous amount of trouble, it was all in vain, she could only get a perfectly uninteresting and commonplace person in glasses, which refused to flatter.'

A few months ago I would have admired these two women living their lives according to their own rules. Now they seemed like children playing a tedious game. While Marianne was there Mrs Cameron also shot some studies of the locals. 'She took such a fancy to the back of one of them (which she said was absolutely superb) that she insisted on her son retaining him as a gardener, though she had no garden and he did not know even the meaning of the word.' I put the book down and took a deep breath. It wasn't just Marianne's casual cruelty, or this vision of well-bred women playing with people like toys; it was the ugly reality of empire that niggled at me the further I waded into her book. Marianne would no doubt have argued that the endeavour was a noble one, intended to bring civilisation and industry to foreign lands. But she embodied the arrogance underpinning the whole concept – the self-belief that allowed not just the British but all colonial powers to go out into the world and take what they wanted at whatever price.

I looked out at my courtyard, the clematis snaking up the mimosa trunk, leaned upon by the branches of the Bengal crimson rose. Without those men crossing oceans and staking claim to land that wasn't theirs, those plants wouldn't be here – and neither would I. That evening I trawled through archives of Mrs Cameron's images, entranced by the soft focus and sepia light, and found one photograph taken during Marianne's stay. The artist sits on a veranda, wearing a formal gown she would have loathed, painting a little boy carrying a water urn. How strange to see her on that island – Serendip to the Arab invaders, Ceilão to the Portuguese, Ceylon to the British – a place that had always been owned. I printed the picture and stuck it on my wall.

8

Messis: The Month of Reaping

I sat in a coffee shop waiting for Chris, a member of the volunteer group who looked after my local park. I had seen groups of people doing odd jobs around the park, watching their slow progress while the toddler scrambled up slides and the baby absorbed the noise and energy of the playground. They were a mixed bunch: bearded men, elderly ladies, children who had been dragged along for fresh air. I felt drawn to them because, unlike for the joggers and the football players, the park wasn't just a backdrop for them, it was the focal point – the reason they came.

On weekends they gathered in the wildlife garden or under the portico by the ornamental flower beds and busied themselves with maintenance jobs or litter collection. The park had done so much to help me in the dark days after the baby was born that I felt a growing compulsion to return the favour. I found a contact email and decided to get in touch. I must have introduced myself to a stranger a million times or more. The spiel was an easy one. 'Hi, I'm a journalist for the *Sunday Times* and I'm writing a piece about so and so.' Now, without that professional armour, I was once more at a loss about how to ask. Who was I and what was I doing? The baby was lying on a cushion beside me, echoing my confusion with an earnest, inquisitive hoot. I would keep it brief, I decided. 'I'm a horticulture student living nearby, I'm off work for a while and I'm keen to get involved.' Chris replied straight away and suggested we meet face to face at the café at the end of my road.

I waited nervously, listening to the hum of chatter around me and the angry whirr of the blender behind the counter, wondering how much I ought to say. He arrived shortly after I did. He was much younger than I had expected, blond-haired with round spectacles which made him look cherubic, though he must have been thirty-five. We acknowledged each other's quizzical expressions and laughed. We chatted politely, ordered coffees, and did our best to feel our way to something substantial through the rigid rules of social norms. It was like an awkward first date. But as the reserve melted I realised he was a wealth of knowledge, not just about the practical side of managing a park and a group of volunteers but about the ideology of green space.

He lived in flat with his husband, in a building next door to the park. He had, it turned out, worked in local government and charities for many years. His greatest achievement had been hatching a plan to turn a derelict market building into a thriving creative space. Gone were the fruit and veg stalls where you could buy yams and plantain. Now it buzzed with trendy art shops and up-market cafes. There was a hint of apology as he told me this. But the experience had taught him how to navigate the turgid waters of local government. He was a fundraising wizard, applying for grants to resurface the sports pitches and helping to devise a master plan for the long-term future of the park. He had an impressive ability to conjure up money where none existed. He was a gifted submitter of grant applications and funding appeals. In just a couple of years the results were extraordinary. The old concrete paddling pool, a firm favourite with local families, had been saved from closure by a committee of volunteers. The nineteenth-century stable block that had once sat a few hundred yards from Ruskin's front door and that had been boarded up for years was now on its way to being restored, with plans to become a community hub, rented by the local mental health hospital to offer recovery courses.

For months he had been lobbying the council to provide one full-time park attendant, rather than the ever-changing maintenance team who appeared every now and then to mow the lawns. I listened to him with admiration until there was pause, and it was my turn to fill it. 'I'm a journalist but I got pregnant by accident and then I got very depressed,' I said, trying to make light of it. 'Things were bad for a while but I started going to horticultural therapy and got hooked,' I continued. 'I don't know what I'm going to do next, but I'd like to help.' Chris listened with interest. 'I've got cancer,' he said when I finished talking. 'It feels a bit weird to blurt it out like that.' Time seemed to hang between us for a beat longer than it should before we both began to laugh. The conversation had veered off in a direction neither of us had predicted and we were now in uncharted territory, pioneers striking out on our own. It was funny, and liberating, and it felt like a good start.

Over the next few months I joined the volunteers whenever I could. Sometimes I brought the boys with me. We built a bird box, we pruned apple trees. We crouched over the soil I'd walked over a hundred times and paid attention to it properly for the first time. The baby could not yet crawl, but relocated himself to piles of mud with supernatural ease. One day I found him sitting in the middle of a vegetable bed quietly destroying the brassica leaves. We planted a bed full of medicinal plants opposite the hospital. The foxglove, for example: the delicious spires of cottage-garden perfection are also an elixir for the heart, enabling it to beat more slowly, powerfully and regularly without requiring more oxygen. *Epimedium grandiflorum*, or horny goat's weed, which hugged the borders like a luxurious blanket, was, predictably, used to treat erectile disfunction and low sexual desire.

The history of medicinal plants was rich with story and myth. The Doctrine of Signatures, which dominated European medical thinking in the sixteenth and seventeenth centuries, held that herbs were given by God to heal human ills and that the use of a plant was indicated by its appearance; thus the mottled ovate leaves of lungwort suggest diseased lungs. Modern medicine is still to a large degree based on knowledge acquired from plants. In some cases the link is more direct. The yew is the sacred tree of Hecate, the Greek goddess associated with witchcraft, death and necromancy. It was said to purify the dead as they entered Hades, and its twisted boughs hold pride of place in many church graveyards today. The leaves and seeds of the plant are lethal if eaten, but the poisonous alkaloid in the leaves is used in medicines. The needles of the English yew are still collected between the months of May and October, the drugs they make helping to stop the division of cancerous cells. 'That makes sense,' Chris said when I told him, 'because cancer drugs feel like being poisoned.'

There were all sorts of characters in these community groups, strong opinions and big personalities which occasionally butted heads. But mostly it was harmonious, a chance to get to know neighbours within the space we shared. Susanne, a quiet woman in her fifties, had gardened a little as an adult, she told me, but she had grown up on a plant nursery in The Republic of Ireland and her family was full of horticulturalists and gardeners. She had been in the capital for over thirty years by the time she joined the volunteers. 'It was only after I got involved with the park that I felt I belonged,' she told me as we lugged wheelbarrows full of rusty old tools and equipment from one corner of the park to the other.

There was no pressure to mingle or chat – companionable silence was good enough, punctuated by regular breaks to eat biscuits and drink tea poured from a thermos flask. The exception to the rule was Chris, who talked incessantly, filling the peace with talk of Labour Party politics, his husband's passion for cycling or his latest plan for the park. It was the perfect soundtrack to work to; he kept up the tempo with his enthusiasm and his ideas.

A charity built an outdoor gym using the steel from knives which had been confiscated by the police. It was a gang-neutral territory and, so the theory went, could be a place where allegiances fell away. We bought a new greenhouse with funds that Chris and the other volunteers had raised, and trained the espaliered apple trees that bordered the community garden like a line of children holding hands. My mind was still as I worked. Digging, planting, moving, letting the soil slip beneath my fingernails – I preferred not to wear gloves because I liked to see this mark of the psychological release taking place in my head. Every park in the area depended on similar armies of volunteers and I began to join them too, determined to turn the ugliness and confusion of the pregnancy into something lasting and valuable instead.

The almshouses I had walked around all those months ago were in one of London's few post-Victorian parks, a vast green space carved out of bomb-damaged housing in the wake of the Second World War. It was surrounded by council tower blocks, some of which were in the process of being knocked down to make way for shiny new developments. The council had spent millions buffing and grooming the space; they had hired a leading landscape architect to plant the beds, created BBQ areas and a sweeping fishing lake. It looked breathtaking during the summer months – white hollyhocks danced up a sunken border, standing shoulder to shoulder with the liquidambar trees, like brides walking down the aisle.

One of the hills had been planted in a naturalistic style – bright-purple spires of salvia nudged their way through ornamental grasses long enough to lose a dog in. Yellow bursts of sea kale exploded from the undergrowth, while the green pods of honesty began to dry and take on the ephemeral quality of silk purse. Dotted throughout were cardoons, great sculptural giants with violet crowns.

People flocked here during the summer from the squeezed apartment buildings nearby; couples came to jog, drunks came to drink. South Asian women picked mugwort for headaches and dandelion leaves to eat. The maintenance of it was another matter. There was one head gardener and a handful of part-time workers battling to care for the 140-acre site. It was a slog – rubbish built up in neglected corners, those dreaded spires of dock sprang up like grim reapers in the flower beds. They would have had to admit defeat long ago without the army of volunteers who came to weed, to prune, to collect the rubbish left behind. I knew what would happen if they did not.

Another green space, once part of a fifty-acre estate attached to a Victorian poorhouse, had been handed over to a supermarket chain to maintain by a local council that lacked the funds. These corporate giants had turned a blind eye as neglect set in; what did they care if the people in the blocks of flats that surrounded it had nowhere to kick a ball, as long as they still went to the superstore to get whatever they needed to eat? I walked around it with the baby in the buggy. 'Hold my hand,' I told the toddler as we pushed our way through the brambles growing thick on each side, the fruit just beginning to form. 'Can I pick?' the toddler asked. There were beer cans and energy drink bottles scattered beneath the bushes like fallen leaves. It was dark and dense, a place where people came to do the things they shouldn't. 'Not from here,' I told him as we turned back to go home.

At the opposite end of the scale were parks that had been tended with love. One of them was a little to the north of my home, in one of those forgotten pockets of the city that is served by neither Tube nor bus. It was designed by Fanny Wilkinson, the first female landscape architect, whose legacy seems to have been missed by almost everyone.

I loved this space. The park, ordered and logical, seemed to take you by the hand the moment you entered it. Walking around it was as soothing as a conversation with the wisest of friends. The wrought-iron gates led to a circular bed which was a head-high haze of fennel, cornflowers the blue of a perfect summer sky and poppies, flashes of red made, so the story goes, from drops of the slain Adonis' blood. Fanny Wilkinson lived in the city at the same time as Marianne and the two women were passionate about many of the same things. She was the daughter of a well-known physician, the eldest of his seven children, and decided early on that she wanted to work with plants.

In the nineteenth century that was easier said than done. Domestic gardening was an acceptable womanly pursuit; running a business that involved design, hard landscaping, dealing with horticultural suppliers, supervising the work of male gardeners and keeping abreast of the accounts was not. Like Marianne, she found a way. She was a friend of Millicent Fawcett and a suffragist in her own right. She was admitted to the Crystal Palace School of Landscape Gardening and Practical Horticulture in 1883, the first woman to have done so and an achievement that had required some grit. Afterwards she was elected honorary landscape gardener to the Metropolitan Public Gardens, Boulevard and Playground Association, and later elected to the Kyrle Society, the organisation founded by Miranda Hill to bring beauty to the lives of the urban poor. I furrowed through archives and libraries looking for any reference to her but there was virtually nothing to be found.

What I did discover was that she was another indomitable figure, a woman who knew her mind. She designed seventy-seven parks in total and demanded recognition on the same level as men. 'I certainly do not let myself be underpaid as many women do,' she said crisply in her one and only interview. 'That I will never do. I know my profession and charge accordingly, as all women should.' I watched the people playing football, the families having birthday parties in the gazebos Wilkinson had put in place. Today this is a high-density urban landscape, surrounded by high-rise towers of flats. Had she ever imagined then how valuable this space would be?

The park took on a greater meaning now that I knew of its creator. As well as order, I saw fortitude in the mulberry trees which were thought to have survived since she put them there. The smaller of the two bandstands was available for hire. One day I peered in and saw a children's party taking place inside while the toddler dug around in a nearby flower bed. The baby and I retreated under the weeping ash, parting its branches like curtains and stepping into the peaceful chamber inside. He looked up, transfixed again by the shifting shadows of dark and light.

The most exciting legacy of Wilkinson's time here was the Victorian greenhouse that had miraculously survived two world wars. It was the park's hub, its beating heart. In the nineteenth century it would have been used to grow the bedding plants that would fill the borders outside. It was still used for this; seeds were planted here, seedlings brought on, some to plant, some to sell, some to give to other community gardening groups nearby. It seemed a sleepy sort of place on first impression, the sort of conservatory that you wanted to curl up inside with a good book. But everything here was moving and growing at an extraordinary pace.

I darted out at lunchtimes with the baby asleep in his pram. I staked tomatoes, pondered the different shapes and smells of the chilli plants. My guide was Naomi, a musician turned gardener who had grown up down the road. We cut open milk bottles, poked holes in plastic yoghurt pots and filled them with herbs. There was nothing that Naomi could not repurpose and find a use for, and soon I started to notice her little touches all over the park – the milk-bottle herb containers that hung outside the café kiosk, the plastic packing crates where tomato plants now grew. She had learned about plants from her mother, who had come from Jamaica many decades before. She had got hold of an allotment and grew the food she missed from home and could not find.

As a child, Naomi had listened with mild disinterest, unaware that one day this knowledge would become her passion and her career. Gardening did that, I noticed; the love for it could lie dormant for many years just like a seed until the conditions were right to wake it up. Now, every Sunday she set a market stall in front of the larger of the Victorian bandstands and sold the vegetables we had grown here to local people.

If anyone was in charge, though, it was Arthur, a slimline eccentric with a passion for Marx. Having trained as a landscape gardener, he had realised that he was not, he said delicately, to everybody's taste so he had thrown himself into community projects instead. His conversation leaped about dizzyingly, from the dangers of the right-wing kleptocracy to the imminent threat of a global famine, all delivered matter-of-factly in an accent that was pure, polished, cut glass. The greenhouse had been kitted out with home-made 'tables' containing layers of soil, Arthur's ingenious invention to maximise the room to grow; he was the mad scientist and the greenhouse was his lab.

The heavy lifting was done by Tefere, as solid and unshakeable as Arthur was feather-light. His father had a 200-hectare farm in Ethiopia and he had learned how to garden there, growing papayas and mangoes on his own little plot. By the time he arrived here, in his thirties, he knew everything about the soil, but his knowledge didn't translate. 'I recognised the cabbages, but I didn't know they were called brassicas,' he chuckled as we potted on some chilli plants. He went to an agricultural college in Suffolk and ended up here as the only paid full-time park attendant the council could afford. He loved it, he told me, and I could see he meant it as I watched him working quietly on busy days. His favourite time, though, was winter mornings when the gates were locked and he stood here in the dark. He could pretend that there was no one else in the city, no one here but him.

Slowly I began to understand what it was that made people do this, what motivated them to come and work here day after day. The need to grow things is hardwired into us: a simple way of showing that we care enough to plan for tomorrow, to leave the world a little better than it was when we arrived. I saw it in the tomatoes growing on cramped windowsills, the runner beans jostling for space on balconies, the pots of herbs placed beside front doors. The need to improve the place we lived in, to cultivate the soil in the heart of a city was as important as it was in the country, maybe more so.

In the middle of a vast housing estate someone had taken a roll-top bath, drilled holes in the bottom and filled it with earth. Pelargoniums grew there now, pinks and purples, their delicate scents wafting out at the people walking past. Awkwardly Chris told me that he would be away for a few weeks, that his cancer treatment would force him from his beloved park. Later I discovered it was stage-four bowel cancer, that time had a different meaning for him. There was nothing mild about making things grow; it was an act of defiance, a way of making your mark on the world.

The baby's appetite was unstoppable now. Whatever I fed him, it was never enough. He ate sweet potatoes, mushed bananas, sticky lumps spilling down his chin. I peeled an avocado and crushed its buttery flesh with a fork. He swallowed a spoonful, opening his little mouth for more. Rolls began to appear on his thighs; I ran my hand over them, enjoyed the generous bounce of his skin, pretended to take a bite out of this glorious fat that had been unimaginable a few months ago.

As he ate and ate, gorging like the hungry caterpillar, his personality continued to grow. After all those months of uncertainty he had found his feet at last and he was determined to take on the world alone. He knew what he wanted and would find a way to get it, whether it was a ball, a breadstick, the urgent need to be picked up and kissed. I recognised him now. This was the child I had felt in my belly all those months before. We sat together in the courtyard, beneath the yellow umbrellas of the bronze fennel-seed heads. I looked at the pots, each containing a different idea or experiment, a bittersweet step towards this day, and I was torn knowing that all too soon it was going to end.

The final day of my maternity leave hovered on the horizon like a guillotine, and I couldn't think of a way to escape the blade. The physical space around me had come into focus, but I was no clearer about what my own life was going to look like now that the boys were both here and the colour and texture of everything had changed. To go back would mean returning to chaos, to risk losing whatever carefully curated order I had built this past year. Even if they still wanted me, I wasn't sure I could see the point when the reality of working life with young children seemed to mean being so strung out you enjoyed nothing at all.

Yet the idea of walking away from the only thing I'd ever really loved doing felt like a different sort of betrayal. Marianne had forgone a personal life for an intellectual one. How could it be that my choices today were more or less the same?

I distracted myself with my evening classes. I did my homework and crammed my head with everything I could learn. I studied soil types and land management. What to do with chalk, sand. I thought I had nailed down the exact definition of loam, only to lose it again. I learned that London was built on clay – thick and cloying – and felt a renewed sense of wonder that every plant I'd seen this year could get what it needed from this.

The land around us had moved in and out of cultivation throughout the years. When the zoological garden closed, it had been bricked over with slum housing and industrial sites. We visited some with George, all of us standing in the sun and shouting out the things we thought you would need to do to bring the land back to life. I learned about the genealogy that divided the plant kingdom into two worlds: that dicotyledons germinated with two seed leaves and monocotyledons, grasses, palms and ferns germinated with one leaf and had come into existence first. They had overlapped with the dinosaurs I spent my evenings helping the toddler trying to identify.

Very, very slowly, I began to recognise the plants and their names – to know that *Asteraceae* had flowers which looked like daisies while *Campanulaceae* had ones that looked like bells. I could see now that the Latin wasn't there to trip me but to help me chart this unfamiliar terrain; a plant with *utilis* in its name was useful or had economic value, while *futilis* meant it had no value at all. *Officinalis*, meaning literally 'of the shop', indicating that it had medicinal properties. *Alba* meant white. *Vulgare* meant common. *Arvensis* told you that a plant was usually found in a field, *sylvestris* that it grew in the wood. *Amophilus* meant it liked the sand. A plant with *salina* in its name would thrive in salty conditions and you would find it by the sea. The names were haphazard, yes, but there was a charm to that. Hints to the plants' personalities had been left like cheat sheets by someone who had observed them centuries ago. I had a soft spot for the night-flowering *Pelargonium triste* with her sad grey-green leaves and for the 'wandering' daisy, *Erigeron peregrinus*, a carefree soul that would self-seed at will. The bay tree was named *Laurus nobilis* as a nod to history and its place on an emperor's crown.

Not only could I now speak the language, however falter-ingly, I had people to practise it with. I bumped into Richard hanging around outside the garages and we walked through the park together hunting in the flower beds to see what we could find. He and Ken went for regular strolls to try to identify the city's trees. I walked the dog with Sarah, talking about very little, but finding her quiet company calming all the same. There were still a few mysteries that eluded me and these I wanted more than ever to figure out. The beautiful flower bed that had cheered me up all those months earlier was not a one-off. I spotted similar patches of harmony, with similar plants and the same style of planting which I knew was not the work of the council's maintenance team. Sometimes they huddled around the base of a kerbside tree; instead of weeds or scrappy grass there were bright-pink flecks of salvia hot lips and the pale-pink faces of erigeron daisies.

The best one of all – the centrepiece, I realised as soon as I saw it – was a largish space at the bottom of a railway bridge. It would have been forgotten by everyone but for one person who wanted to make it sing. The mystery gardener had transformed it into a roadside spectacle. Roses were trained up against the brick wall, echiums and a palm tree beside them, a clematis running up its trunk like a ribbon. In the bed itself the concave cups of the canna lilies shone like flames over a mass of shiny, generous fatsia leaves. White spikes of acanthus interrupted the show, beaming like the Eiffel Tower at night. The slender arcs of the *Salvia 'Amistad'* rose up, a fleet of ships with their sails at full mast. The flamboyant reds of the hollyhocks swirling in the middle were flamenco dancers lifting their skirts. It was a celebration of life itself. I made detours just to be able to stop and drink it in. 'It's the best therapy, isn't it?' a builder shouted as he walked by.

We think of depression and anxiety as diseases of modern life, but nervous conditions swept Britain in the seventeenth and eighteenth centuries. The Industrial Revolution shook the country and changed the way we lived. Work no longer followed daylight hours; cities boomed, and office culture set in. A delicate constitution was something to be proud of at the time, a sign of the refined nature of a true gentleman. In 1733 George Cheyne published *The English Malady*, grouping together vague conditions such as lowness of spirit, spleen and vapours which were 'scarce known to our ancestors, and never r[ose] to such fatal heights, nor afflict[ed] such numbers in any other known nation'.

Over the next century the pressure grew to achieve one's full potential. Victorian society fetishised productivity, discrediting lethargy and incapacitation. Moral obedience was an essential requirement and often came at a terrible cost. Marianne's brother-in-law, the literary critic John Addington Symonds, was a well-known example. He met Catherine, Marianne's sister, in Switzerland in 1863 having fled a scandal at Magdalen College, Oxford, where he was a Fellow. His homosexuality and uncon-summated love affairs were a recurrent theme of his work and he suffered from ongoing periods of depression. At the time they met, he had been accused of pursuing a young man and fled to Switzerland suffering from 'stress'. He married Janet, as she was known to family, in Hastings despite the scandal and they went on to have four daughters together.

Marianne did not approve of the match, but his mental health was not the reason. Like the Georgians, the Victorians were broadly accepting of 'nervous' conditions. Complaints like melancholia and shattered nerves were common diagnoses and were generally considered to be the result of an underlying phys-ical cause, an illness that could not be helped. That started to change in the twentieth century, when Freudian psychoanalysis and changes in the medical profession led people to believe that mental illness was purely psychological and due to a weakness in the sufferer's character.

Marianne herself was suffering from psychological tremors that sounded eerily familiar. I had picked up the book again reluctantly after a pause of a month or more. It would have been easier to stop reading, to put her *Recollections* back on the shelf and get on with life, but she was making me think about the world in a way I had not before.

Marianne was not a heroine in a novel, she was a real person who was nuanced and flawed. The period she lived through was every bit as complicated as she was; it was a time of awesome achievements and despicable acts, of empowerment and oppression, of constantly conflicting tides. What I felt about it was irrelevant; it had happened and the impact of it was everywhere I looked. I saw it in language and landscape, in literature and politics, in myself and the millions like me, people whose identities are divided, both coloniser and colonised.

Besides, I was curious. Marianne had captured my attention and I wanted to know what happened next. It was 1883 and she had set off for the Seychelles to paint the Coco de Mer palm in its natural habitat. The tree's nut, the largest in the world, was highly prized and rare. Its shape, resembling a woman's buttocks and thighs, had made it the subject of endless rumours. Malay seamen believed that the trees grew on the seabed in underwater forests; others argued that the male trees, which grow large, phallic catkins, uprooted themselves on stormy nights and made love to female trees, but anyone who witnessed them would go blind. Marianne viewed this with as much amusement as she had her phallic stinkhorn mushroom all those years ago: in other words, none at all.

She did the Victorians proud, painting and writing about it without once giving in to innuendo. I felt her raising an eyebrow at me coolly as I laughed. She set off from Marseilles, sharing the ship with 'four most remarkable donkeys on their way to New Caledonia to found a race of noble quadrupeds as yet unknown in those distant islands'. She arrived without incident, was welcomed at Government House and promptly set off for an expedition to locate a cocoa nut with six heads. It was an ugly deformity, she wrote, but a good excuse for a walk. She dismissed the chair and bearers who had been sent to accompany her ('I found the men were greatly in my way'), trekking past breadfruit trees loaded with fruit and twisted cashew trees, their long arms spread over the sand, until she found her goal.

She explored the islands thoroughly, travelling between them by rowing boat in trips that took eleven hours or more. I don't know what she did about food or toilets – she did not bother to say. She found a dilapidated paradise on the island of Curieuse, a place inhabited by one old Englishman and a leper colony, one of only two places where the Coco de Mer grows wild. The one she painted, which I recognised from the walls of her gallery at Kew, had twenty-six nuts upon it. Her description of the plant is unusually abrupt: 'the outer shell was green and heart-shaped; only the inner shell was double, and full of white jelly, enough to fill the largest soup tureen'. At Christmas the whole population got mad drunk. 'It was like the island of lunatics and we barred all the windows before going to bed,' she wrote. For the first time I began to feel sorry for Marianne, out there on her own. What was she doing it for? She had confused intimacy with weakness, privilege with superiority and I still wasn't sure what it was that she wanted to prove.

By the time she was ready to return to England she was not allowed to board the boat. There had been an outbreak of small-pox and thirteen deaths, so she agreed to a period of quarantine before she could leave. The first ten days passed well enough. She painted continually, looking out at the lovely views and marvellous colours of the sea. But after that her mind became troubled. Some of the inmates took to playing tricks on her and she thought that they would rob or murder her.

For two days she barricaded the window and was in fear of her life, hearing things said behind the low divisions which others told her never had been said. 'Doctors say my nerves broke down from insufficient food and overwork in such a climate.' The ship came at last, but the voices continued all the way back to England. She recovered from this episode but would suffer from bouts of 'nerves' for the rest of her life, hearing voices which taunted her and told her she was worthless. She called them 'the enemy', these constant noises. She couldn't escape them in London, or anywhere else. The plants she painted were the only release; they comforted her and reassured her, they helped the world to make sense.

9

Exsolationis: The Month of Sowing

I was standing in a stranger's doorway in south London, talking to a woman in a pale-blue nightdress and slippers. 'They call me a guerrilla gardener!' Gloria chuckled, and I couldn't quite believe that I had found her. This was the woman who had been planting exquisite patches of greenery around the streets I'd been walking through all year.

The day was steamy, the air as thick as it was at closing time. The baby and I were on our way to the garden when we took a detour to admire my favourite bed. It was past its best now, unbuttoned and louche. The acanthus that had looked fierce was beginning to pale, the silver petals falling to reveal the tiny, sealed mouths of seed heads. The salvias were no longer blowing jubilant in the breeze; they drooped a little, looking as tired and uncomfortable as I was. But there was beauty in the tangle of colours, something exquisite in the defiant mood of the bed as the summer began to fade away.

The baby was facing forwards in the buggy now so he too could admire the scene. He no longer needed to see me in front of him as we walked; in fact he objected to it, crying for a more stimulating view. Just as I was preparing to leave I felt someone looking at me from behind. I turned and there she was, standing on the doorstep of a Victorian terraced house, her proud smile giving her away. I waved and made my way towards her, grateful that the baby was there to give me an appearance of sanity as I hurtled across the road.

'Do you know who does this?' I asked, pushing the buggy across the street to her front door. 'Why?' she asked with a smile.

'Because it's beautiful and I've been wondering if I could do it too.'

She chuckled. 'Once you start it will hit you here,' she said, patting the palm of her hand against my chest. 'People will sleep in it. They'll take the things you plant there, throw rubbish inside. It will hurt you and, I'm telling you, you won't be able to stop.'

I had always known that those beds weren't the work of a gardener employed by the council, that this was something someone did on their own initiative, out of love, on land that did not belong to them. For months I had been wondering who this secret plantsman or woman might be. What sort of person spent their spare time tending to beds that no one else cared for, in corners of the city that were otherwise ignored? Who chose to express their passion in this way?

It had occurred to me that it might be a professional gardener, a green-fingered revolutionary, one of the eco warriors from the squat nearby. Somehow Gloria made more sense. The un-selfconscious mood of the planting, the raucous celebration of the beds, suited her very well. I stood on the porch and grilled her in a way I hadn't grilled anyone for months. She was born in Barbados, in Bathsheba, where the cold water of the Atlantic clashes with the warmth of the Caribbean Sea. She had grown up surrounded by palms, star fruit and the majestic grandeur of the cotton tree. It was the same lush tropical greenery that inspired Marianne to set out on her own journey across the sea. Cultivating the soil was instinctive in a climate like that, where gardens were like sweet shops – full of delicious treats. Gloria had moved to this corner of south London thirty years earlier, long before the new developments started to go up. The iron bars on windows and cages on front doors were reminders of what this area had once been. But Gloria had seen beyond all that; to her it was home.

Opposite her ground-floor flat was a large bank of earth cornering the railway arch. It was full of old mattresses, broken chests of drawers. She called the council and asked them to clear it away. At first they ignored her, but Gloria persevered. She called and called, wrote to them and eventually they came and cleared the rubbish away. She had a blank slate then. Admittedly, it was one that no one else wanted, but that didn't bother her at all. She began to plant things, filling it up bit by bit. Most of it she grew from seed, lining up the pots on the bay window of her sitting room until the seeds germinated in the spring sun.

One year she tried roses, the next it was foxgloves. Sometimes it didn't quite work, things were taken, and for a while she gave up. But the next year she'd be back again puzzling over seed catalogues, gathering cuttings, looking for the perfect fit. She came up against councils and vandals, and a man who slept on her camellia for six months. Every obstacle made her more determined to make that patch of land thrive. As the bed became more spectacular, the backdrop to it began to gentrify. The overflowing skips were replaced with neat bin stores, front doors were repainted as flats were sold and professional couples moved in. Gloria had been right – there was value in this rundown corner of London where labourers had lived for over 200 years. Now the meaning of the planting changed; it was no longer an act of defiance, it was something that brought the neighbourhood together, the perfect backdrop to the annual summer fete. The land belonged to the railway company, Gloria told me, and eventually they came knocking, asking her to pay for the right to plant there. By then the flower beds had become such a focal point that the other residents pooled together and formed an association to fund and maintain her handiwork.

Over the years she had learned what worked and what didn't. She liked hardy geraniums, echiums which looked so outlandish they were entirely at home against the tired brickwork of the Victorian railway arch. There was a palm tree of some sort standing proudly in the background. Soon other people wanted to do the same. A young couple stopped by to ask for tips and she started to notice their efforts in beds and tree pits nearby. It was a secret network of people reinvigorating their streets. 'The trick is to plant things that self-seed and take care of themselves,' she told me. I saw the feathered leaves of cosmos; tough plants despite their delicate air, they kept going all summer with no need for maintenance. The lush green leaves of *Fatsia japonica* gave the bed a tropical air. She wasn't a snob when it came to flowers, as city gardeners rarely were. They were interested in practicalities like endurance; they needed plants that could thrive in smog and dust. Pink and purple geraniums popped up like glow sticks, violas self-seeded and salvias bounded through the bed with simple, joyful strides.

My mind was buzzing when I left her. I had been feeling some of the old turbulence in the past few days. I lay awake at night worried and tense; guilty that I was still in a limbo; guilty that I couldn't just make up my mind about what to do next. I tested out fantastical futures where I set up a gardening business, where we all moved out of the city and I worked outdoors. I was a woeful cliché, and I knew it. Until now I'd only had one goal to work towards: my own intellectual satisfaction. Now I just wasn't sure it was worth the strife.

As I floundered on like a gap-year student, the baby was taking control. He had changed beyond recognition – the discomfort of those earlier months was long gone. These days he observed Bev with critical interest. He was fascinated by trees, buses, pigeons, but nothing captivated him quite as much as people. He was more sociable than I could believe, as though the months we'd spent cocooned in green spaces had given him an insatiable appetite for human company instead.

He smiled beatifically at strangers. If this failed to elicit a response he tried raspberries, blowing them with theatrical delight. The NHS therapy sessions I had been going to, having finally made it to the front of the queue, were inevitably interrupted as he babbled and chatted to the therapist until she couldn't help but laugh. I listened as she talked about balance: how everyone needed an equal amount of duty, work and fun, and I realised how fortunate I had been to stumble across Marianne all those months ago. Would I have discovered any of this if I hadn't walked into her gallery and seen the world through her eyes?

The baby's joy in being alive was now as all-consuming as the black cloud that had smothered me when he was born. I watched him flirt with strangers on the bus, fix his eyes upon a middle-aged man in a suit and coo cheerfully until he dissolved into laughter. I was superfluous, there simply for structural support. The love I felt for him now was as invasive and unstoppable as the weeds that sprang from the city walls. That the parks had incubated us was obvious. There was no doubt in my mind that they had done as much to get us started as the doctors at the hospital who had delivered him.

I felt proprietorial as I walked through them now; they were our garden, our playgroup and nursery, the place where we both felt most at home. The idea of urban parks is as old as cities themselves. The ancient Romans called it *rus in urbe* – bringing the countryside into the city. The essayist and gardener John Evelyn expanded on this in the seventeenth century, when he proposed a series of parks and gardens around London to relieve the city smog. He suggested planting honeysuckle, jasmine, lilac and lavender, highly scented plants that would through their 'innocent magic' reduce the sulphurous sea of coal smoke that filled the air.

But it wasn't until the mid-nineteenth century that the first civic parks were built as a way of giving the urban poor a release from the grind of city life. There was an urgent public-health need, not that you would know it from Marianne's account of London at the time. Cholera and tuberculosis broke out in slum areas like the one where the garden stood, just across the river from the white-stucco building where she and her father lived. The poor needed to breathe fresh air. But green spaces provided something more as well. Pioneers of the urban parks movement, like Edwin Chadwick, Robert Peel and Octavia Hill, believed that access to nature was essential, not just to stop the spread of disease in city slums but for quality of life. Towards the end of the nineteenth century, physicians began to theorise that it was urban life itself that was fuelling the rise in nervous conditions.

In 1881 the American doctor and neurologist George Miller Beard coined the term 'neurasthenia' to describe a dizzying range of symptoms from fatigue, anxiety and headaches to impotence and depression. These were a direct result of urban living, he believed, said to stem from overstimulation, overexertion, over-indulgence and an increasingly competitive atmosphere. Stated simply, people were attempting to achieve more than their constitution could cope with. The cure was withdrawal from the pressures of urban life, rest and a simpler, healthy lifestyle. The concept spread throughout Europe. In England parks were a 'living tonic' that could help to cure a wide range of nervous conditions; foliage was believed to be able to disinfect the air while providing relief to body and mind. Physicians prescribed walks in these new 'green lungs' to anxious and exhausted patients. The perceived health benefits of green spaces fuelled the park movement. In the UK, more public parks opened between 1885 and 1914 than ever before or since.

But the city has kept on growing. I walked through the large park to the north of the house, where the almshouses stood, and tried to imagine what it had looked like 200 years before. The Grand Surrey Canal ran through connecting warehouses and around it, tenements provided slum housing for the labourers to live in. Now it was clear and verdant, a place to breathe freely and escape the city noise. Bald patches marked the lawn. Dried spires of *Veronicastrum* shot out of it like the contrails of an aeroplane. The round heads of the hydrangeas were blanching and fading from blue-back to creamy white. Tangles of dry sea kale covered the hillside, interrupted by tufts of sky-blue heather and the umbels of cow parsley had flipped inside out like umbrellas in the gale. The value of these spaces was awesome. Not just to the people in the high-rises next door, where the balconies were crammed with bicycles and buggies, possessions they needed and couldn't fit indoors, but also for the city's other inhabitants, the orange-tipped butterflies which stepped delicately across the Queen Anne's lace, the bats that hunted here, the moths and frogs and crows that watched me passing, respectfully dipping their heads.

It was remarkable what nature could forgive when you allowed it to. To the north of the park was a site which had once been toxic: the refuse wharf at the end of the canal, opposite the gramophone factory owned by Edison Bell. Now it was a city farm where people grew produce for local businesses on beds created from mounds of soil piled on waste logs, cushioned with chopped weeds, old cardboard and manure. Some plants can actively remove poisons from the soil; sunflowers were used to extract radioactive isotopes from the exclusion zone around Chernobyl. Ferns can do the same with arsenic; brassicas extract lead.

The parks were quieter now that the season had shifted and the schools had started. I was back behind my desk as well; a new term of evening classes at the garden had begun. Unlike at real school, I felt pure joy that I could return to work. I studied diagrams that reminded me of GCSE biology, only this time they made sense: pistil, stigma, ovary, pollen. There were new faces in the classroom, new students had joined, replacing those who had finished their year, gained a qualification and left. No one ever went willingly; terms ended not with elation but with sadness as happy students were shoved unwillingly out of the classroom door.

Some went on to be freelance gardeners, others joined private landscaping firms. A few took part in trainee schemes in Royal Parks. One classmate came back with plans to a start a business, using the waste on a nearby estate to make compost to sell back to the residents.

The party was winding down outside the classroom too. Only the most determined refused to let go of the fun. The trumpet vine had conquered the neighbouring wall of the army barracks, its bright-red flowers like a victorious flag over the battlefield below. Beneath them the red-hot pokers swivelled their heads over the beds like parrots and in the corner the brugmansia lounged, hanging its pendulous orange flowers like lanterns in an opium den, their delicate smell intensifying in the evenings in the hope of tempting the pollinator moths. I knew this because Marianne had seen the same plant in Brazil all those years before.

The perennial wallflowers had given up their multicoloured rapture, the stately heads of the cardoons were now as white as King Lear's mane. It wasn't sadness that struck me as I walked around the garden, but a feeling of fulfilment. They had achieved what they came for and now they were approaching the inevitable end. The purpose of the spectacle I'd admired all year was simple: to make sure another generation was on the way. In this way nature was like a good Asian mother, always worrying about the offspring coming further down the line. Yolk-coloured flowers were replaced by fat-bellied pumpkins lurking beneath saucepan-shaped leaves. Pears ripened. Olives grew and the espaliered apple trees, heavy with fruit like pregnant women, rested their weary backs against the wall. George was triumphant. These apple trees had stopped fruiting several years before. Perhaps they'd got tired of the noise, been stressed by the city smog. Now they had finally agreed to forgive and move on.

The scene was less eye-catching, but it was a mistake to look away. It was only after the bombast of summer that plants revealed how they worked and why. Berries in lurid and surprising shades of yellow and purple were there to tempt the birds. Just like the crab apples and swollen hips on the roses, they were mobile dispersal units to scatter seed in distant pavement cracks and roads. The dogwood Sarah picked from Bear's coat had evolved so that squirrels and foxes could wander and spread its seeds far away. Some travelled in water, others relied on wind. Umbels of fennel were held flat like an open palm, hoping their seed would catch the breeze. The stately hornbeam that guarded the perimeter of the garden showered the lawn with aerodynamically perfect helicopter pods like rain. I picked them up and carried them home with me, letting the boys drop them out of their bedroom window and watch them fly down to the street below.

For Marianne, too, the seasons were shifting and she was contemplating a new project of her own. It was 1879 and I had joined her once more. She had spent a year in India, drawn to the vast subcontinent by the flora, but by somebody else as well. In the years since they had met on the steamer, she and Dr Burnell had become firm friends. They wrote regularly and, much as she had in her father, she confided in him. She arrived at his house in Tanjore on Christmas Eve, catching him off guard 'as he was sitting amongst his books, deep in work' having expected her on a later train.

The two of them quickly fitted into a happy rhythm. Living with Burnell was 'like living with a live dictionary and made a delightful change', she writes, with undisguised joy. He filled an upstairs bedroom with botanical books and she spent hours poring over them. The two of them explored the area together, she painting and he writing by her side.

She had arrived in India in the middle of a famine, though once again she did not dwell on the human suffering she saw. 'Starvation, flood and fever were all around,' she wrote. 'Everyone was taking opium, so I followed the fashion, prevention being better than cure.' By the time she dragged herself away from the city to continue her journey through India, she and Burnell had made plans to collaborate on a book of sacred Hindu plants together. She left with a list of them in her hand and spent the next fifteen months tracking each one down.

Most of them flowered between March and April in Bengal. From Kerala she travelled by steamer to Bombay and on to Lonavala. She wished to see the Karli Caves. There she was amazed by an ashoka (*Saraca indica*) flower growing through honeycomb. 'I have painted it so,' she wrote to Burnell, 'and you may write a romance about it if you will.' She returned to their project over and over again as she travelled. In June she was 'much provoked on returning to Seharumpore [Saharanpur] to find two of my sacred plants had flowered . . . Now be good and write how you are and how my book is getting on – I love so much to know about the plants – I have only 6 more to do.'

By mid-July she reports: 'I have done all your plants but the two Acacias, Catechu and Soma . . . I long to see your account of them all.' Her hopes for the two remaining plants rested on Calcutta. She arranged a few days' stay en route to Darjeeling, but heavy rains got in the way. She didn't reach Calcutta until September. With the sacred-plant paintings complete, Marianne awaited Burnell's proposed text. After several months she sent a gentle reminder: 'write me word here how you are and how do the sacred plants get on?'.

But Burnell's health – never strong – was failing after a serious attack of cholera; he may have been suffering from partial paralysis at the time she wrote. As his health faded, their plan did as well. She never received his text. She returned to London as free and as aimless as she had been before and put on an exhibition of her paintings in Conduit Street. It garnered so much attention that she was summoned to meet her hero, Charles Darwin. Marianne believed him to be 'the greatest man living, the most truthful as well as the most unselfish and modest, always trying to give others rather than himself the credit of his own great thoughts and work,' she concluded breathlessly. A whole chapter of the book is solemnly titled 'Charles Darwin' to emphasise the gravity of the honour. He advised her that her 'representation of the vegetation of the world' would not be complete until she had visited Australia, where the plant life was radically different from anything he had seen elsewhere. She took this as a 'royal command' and began to plan her next journey straight away.

First, though, she wanted to test out an idea; she wrote to Burnell, tentatively raising it. 'I should like to build a Gallery close to the pleasure grounds (or in them) at Kew, hang my pictures and have coffee and tea for all the poor tired visitors – with a cottage attached to boil the kettle in – and a spare room for myself to go and sulk and paint in when I want rest and green trees. Do you think it will ever come to pass?'

A little later, having missed a train at Shrewsbury station, she wrote a letter to Joseph Hooker at Kew. It was the same letter I had tried to decipher in her gallery all those months before. She offered to leave the gardens her entire collection of paintings and to build a gallery in which to house them, as well as a guardian's house nearby. Hooker agreed and Marianne got to work. She hired James Fergusson, an architect whose work she had encountered in India, and chose a spot as far away from the main entrance as she could find. It was not supposed to be easy to find, intended instead for 'those who cared sufficiently for plants to have made their way through all the houses'. Those who cared only for 'promenading', she sniffed, 'would probably never get beyond the palm house'.

She also obtained permission to build a small studio space for herself or any other artist in which to paint. 'There was no quiet room in the gardens in which a specimen could be copied away from the sloppy greenhouses and traffic of visitors,' she complained. The only sticking point was the refreshments, which Hooker vetoed on the basis that it would be impossible to cater to the 77,000 visitors the gardens received on a busy bank holiday and to the 'difficulty of keeping the British public in order'.

Now, with the wheels in motion, she set off on her travels again. Once more her persistence seemed to have wormed its way into the back of my head like a sharp kick through time. I tried to escape her by taking the baby for a walk through our park on a balmy late-summer afternoon. The grass was parched and a golden retriever strolled through it in a comical echo of a lion through the Serengeti.

Only the swampy surroundings of the wildlife garden remained lush and alive. Raspberries were growing around the edges of the pond and a young crab-apple tree had burst into life. There was a tag attached to its trunk: 'To Mum, the robins in the park will keep you near.' However many times I walked around the park I always found something new – the echo of another person who had followed the same path.

The pond was more of a puddle now and the Canada geese picked their way through the cracked earth looking hot and cross. Beside it the leaves of the Chinese corkscrew willow curled up like ringlets of hair in the humidity of the late-summer sun. We walked through the pergola, where the cascades of wisteria had been replaced with the more peculiar beauty of their velvety-soft seed pods. From the top of the park, I looked back at the city centre again – the glass-tower monoliths and the cranes, vast machines that seemed delicate on the horizon.

I tried to imagine what it would feel like to go back: to leave the house in the dark, walk to the train station and queue shoulder to shoulder for the morning commute. I tried to imagine myself getting on the train – moving at high speed from a world of green to one that was brown, silver and grey, and for the first time I felt a pull to return. As though reading my mind, the baby chattered, dragging me back to the moment and back to him.

We made our way through the familiar contours of this home from home. I found myself back at the carnival tree and ducked under the canopy of leaves. It was a pin oak, a young tree I thought, compared to the vast horse chestnuts and planes that filled the park. I had looked it up online some months before and discovered what it was here for. Three teenage boys had been killed in a road accident the summer they finished school, the news reports said. This tree must have been significant in some way. Hearts hung from the branches, glass baubles, laminated cards with their names written on. Perhaps they had climbed it as children, played football around it during the holidays. Maybe they had brought their first girlfriends here and said the words 'I love you' to someone who wasn't their mum.

Rain had washed the writing from most of the ribbons, but on some the messages remained. 'It started, then it stopped, it was a heart no one forgot.' The world was full of stories that needed telling and I knew in my gut that I still wanted to be part of that.

I resumed my hunt for green spaces and the people who put them there with a new sadness now that I knew these wanderings were coming to an end. For months now I had heard tantalising whispers of a gated garden somewhere nearby. It was open to local residents for a token fee. The associated website crashed, emails went unanswered. But my interested in solving puzzles had been rekindled and I was determined to find out more. I dug out the details from the Charity Commission and found a mobile number for one of the trustees.

If he was surprised to hear from me, in the middle of his workday, in an air-conditioned office somewhere in the city, he didn't let it show. He told me there was a nominal fee of £5 to have a key cut, and a small annual contribution to the upkeep of the park. Then he gave me an address. The secretary lived in an unassuming Victorian semi at the top of the hill. I arrived in the middle of the children's bedtime, forms in hand, and she took them without a glance, distractedly handing me a key. I wanted to ask her about this garden's history – who had created it, who maintained it now – but I could see it wasn't the right time. How long has it been there? I asked instead. 'I don't know, I'm sorry. It's all on the website, I'm afraid,' she replied, edging towards the stairs.

I took the boys up there the following day. It was tucked away at the top of a hill, parallel to the park I'd been going to for months now. Only in London did the contours of wealth change so quickly; up here huge, detached houses stood in the middle of expansive gardens protected from the street by red-brick walls. It was only a ten-minute walk from the kebab shops and takeaways at the other end of the Georgian terrace, but it felt a million miles away. The garden was tucked in the middle of this, hidden away behind a gated door. We walked up a strip of tarmac, past a climbing hydrangea whose petals were parched and already turning the colour of burnished gold. The buddleia, too, had lost the lilac colour from its fuzzy floral brushes, while beside it the friendly leaves of a fig tree greeted me as if to signal that it, at least, was just coming into its own.

I stopped and pointed it out to the boys, reaching up on my tiptoes for the softer fruit near the top of the tree; my fingers could just grasp one which was turning from green to a deep maroon, the skin beginning to sag and give way. I tore it in half and tasted the soft pink flesh, enjoying the surprising sweetness beneath the ugly exterior as I placed a piece into each of their mouths. The tarmac gave way to an old basketball court, the concrete cracked and warped. Beyond it was the sort of space that no longer exists in cities: two acres of wilderness overrun with ivy and makeshift dens. I turned back to look in the direction we'd come from. Behind us was a fence covered with bindweed and runner beans, scrambling their way up from the order of the allotment plots beyond, and in front of that a white-stucco building, grand and serene in this surprising scene.

There was nothing manicured about this space. Nature had been left to take control. The toddler was in paradise rooting around in the undergrowth, a mass of tangled vines and brambles, blackberries ripening on spiky stems. Seven wobbly tree stumps had been placed in a circle. The toddler tried to jump from one to the other, while the baby and I sat in the shade of the trees. It seemed remarkable that this place had avoided property developers and health and safety legislation. That it existed in the middle of a city at all.

IO

Defoliationis: The Month of Falling Leaves

It was autumn now and the echiums split the horizon like pyramids in the sand. The liquidambar tree had turned a burning
gold and the vegetables had bolted. The sky was a dirty grey,
mirroring the pavement beneath.

I was at the garden with the baby, turning a poppy head
upside down and watching the seeds fall out like grains of salt.
I did my best to stop them spreading, running a hand across the
tabletop and scooping them into the palm of my hand. He shook
them like a rattle, dispersing them around him in a fine shower.
It was the vivid red of the poppy's petals that Ruskin had so
admired. With Victorian understatement he said the fine flowers
reminded him of a scarlet cup, a flame, a ruby, a burning coal

fallen from heaven's altars and painted glass – for it never glows so brightly as when the sun shines through it.

For me the humble seed heads were the most sublime. As the plant dried a series of tiny holes opened up in its core, releasing 300,000 seeds to the wind; each seed could lie dormant for eighty years before the right combination of conditions woke it up.

We each had a different seed to gather. Sarah had the spiked pink casing of the castor oil plant – a lurid ball like a toy the toddler would pick from the shelf. The seeds inside had the green metallic sheen of a beetle's shell, every bit as beautiful and surprising as pearls. They were poisonous if you ate too many. Eight was the tipping point, George had told us with such confidence that I forgot to ask how on earth he knew. Delphine had marigolds. Seeds seem to reveal the inner characteristics of a plant; some, like beans, were fat and no-nonsense. Strawberries were impossibly fine, like particles of dust. Others, like marigolds, made no sense at all. These uncomplicated, cheerful flowers had seeds like little shrunken crescents; they looked ancient – miniature fossils excavated after thousands of years.

There was a ceremonial quality to the shaking and sweeping, the gathering of these tiny fragments which would each create a new life. Today the task felt more meditative than usual. I had missed several weeks of therapy and discovered that, in my absence, Helen had died. The last time I had seen her she had been her usual gruff self, wrapped once more in her olive-green coat as summer slipped away and the temperature began to drop.

I had only ever known her in this garden, and the backdrop had suited her very well. Anne told me that Helen had enjoyed her last session – weeding or pruning, I forget which. The following day she had gone to visit a National Trust garden that she loved. Her son had visited for tea and she had gone to have a lie-down after he left. She hadn't woken up again.

Anne told us what she knew about Helen's life. She had been a journalist in the 1950s before her children were born. She tried to keep going, carrying her first baby into the office in a bassinet and parking him under her desk while she typed, but the two worlds had been incompatible. She retrained as a teacher and moved to Africa, where a different kind of adventure had taken shape. There were things I would have liked to ask Helen if I'd met her before her mind had started to roam. Had she ever regretted her decision to change course like that? Had she missed her work? Or found another kind of fulfilment instead? Then I remembered the icy blast of her disapproval and realised that she would have told me to get a grip.

We finished collecting seeds and the usual disorder resumed. Delphine wandered past in front of me, free of supervision, and began to pull chard and chicory out of the raised beds, chatting benignly to herself as she went. Sarah was tidying up the chaos of the potting shed, Bear beside her, surveying the upheaval around him with a fatigued air. He too was dressed for winter, wearing a green woollen jumper with a neat white collar, knitted especially by the woman who lived next door. The garden had grown up without me even noticing it and now it entered a more dignified stage of life. The recklessness of summer had been replaced by a quiet sort of beauty.

The brugmansia had released those trumpet flowers, letting each of them drop, spinning to the floor, but the foliage beneath was bright and alive. A wave of bright-blue salvia 'Super Trooper' (the names I still found hard to forgive) swept over the top of the pumpkins, now pendulous and ready to drop. Nasturtium leaves still fizzed and frothed, tumbling over the sides of the vegetable beds, though their jaunty flowers had been packed away. The soft white buds of the *Magnolia grandiflora* were pushing through now, emerging from the darkness, a partial eclipse of the moon at the end of every branch; and then there was the banana, still looking deliriously out of place as it swayed over the damp, dark city beneath.

Seed heads were an amateur botanist's dream, full of clues for anyone who took the time to look. Anything in the pea family, including lupins and wisteria, formed seeds in a pod which split, firing their hard bullets on to the soil. Members of the cabbage family, *Brassicaceae*, have papery membranes between the two halves, silky divisions like honesty's outer shell. The nettle family, *Lamiaceae*, don't have a pod at all but four seeds on pads at the bottom of the open flower head. Some produce pods on the stalk side of the flower, others in the middle of the flower itself. Each one told you about how this plant had adapted so that it could survive and spread – whether by wind or water or beast.

The dynamics of the group had shifted. Sofia had left a few weeks earlier. She was starting an English course which she hoped would help her to find her way at work. We had eaten cake together as we said goodbye, the conversation unusually stilted as she tried her hardest not to cry. Two new members had joined the therapy group at the garden. Alice, an NHS nurse who had been off with depression for the past year, and Jo, who worked in a café and lived in a campervan because she couldn't afford London rents. Both had the numb, dazed expression I remembered all too well. Jo told me that she hung tillandsias, tentacled air plants that could live without soil, above her sink to remind her of the outdoors. She did not 'do well in cities' she said. We spanned six generations now, this group of women who came here to play in the mud.

I walked with them around the garden as Bev took them on her usual tour. They asked questions and I felt quietly trium-phant as I realised that I now knew the answers. My role here had changed: I was a caretaker, an admirer, a volunteer and a friend. I felt proprietorial towards it, proud of how spectacular it remained. In pots along the pathway were the offshoots of the banana that I had delicately severed from the mother plant, waiting to spend their first winter indoors. The runner beans we had planted in class stuck their heads coyly above the soil and the new tree fern I had dug a hole for and planted a few weeks earlier was sprawling merrily by the classroom door.

Fat bumblebees staggered from flower to leaf, and a snail hitched a ride on my hand as I tiptoed to refill the bird feeder. The temperature dropped and I retreated more and more often into the potting shed and the greenhouses, inhaling the earthy smell that still made me light-headed the moment I opened the door. Just by the entrance to the large greenhouse was a big terracotta pot full of marigolds that Helen had planted the spring before and I could picture her, stooped and smiling with a wicked twinkle in her eye. The person she reminded me of was Marianne. Both were ferocious and defiant but they were vulnerable at the same time. Helen had been born thirty years after Marianne had died and the world had lurched forwards at a dizzying pace since then. I thought about all the progress, the cars, the machinery, the technology, the screens and wondered if the world was really a more hospitable place?

I walked on through the greenhouses, inspecting the coils and tentacles of the pitcher plants that still felt to me like a living incarnation of Marianne, and thought about the conversation I would have to have the next day. I had capitulated, finally, after almost a year of silence and set a date to meet my boss for lunch. I thought about these women who had fascinated and impressed me, and I felt a steeliness creep through me as I watered the plants in the greenhouse and settled them in for the night.

Nothing in nature ended without something else beginning. The seeds we were collecting from the beds would be tucked away in a cool, dark cupboard until the spring. Some would stir the moment they were placed once more in the damp soil and heated by the first rays of the sun. Others needed something dramatic to jolt them into life – a soak in some water, a scrape with a knife – before they would put out roots again. For others, only destruction would do the job. Australian bushfires looked cataclysmic on the evening news, but for banksias and eucalyptus they signalled a new beginning. Even as the fire burned down the trees it melted the resin on the casing of their fruit and pine cones, releasing the seeds within. Other plants required the chemical signals from smoke and charred plant matter to wake them.

I walked home slowly, saying hello to the new cast of characters which had appeared from the wings. Some were familiar. I now knew that those yellow crowns I'd seen at Kew a year earlier were mahonia, a dependable winter highlight of the English gardener. The leaves were thorny, but the rows of tiny yellow flowers blurred together to look like liquid gold. The crocuses that had lifted my spirits in spring had cousins who preferred the gentler temperatures at this time of year. The colour reminded me of the lotus flowers that I had seen in Sri Lanka. The crocus was not English either, but it looked at home here; it was neater and more modest, flowering only briefly as though reluctant to hog the limelight for too long. This brevity only added to its value; the bright-red stigmas inside the *Crocus sativas* were the origin of saffron, the dye that coloured Buddhist monks' robes, the most expensive spice in the world.

The next day I woke up early and fed the baby, talking him through my plans for the day. Lunch with my boss meant the two of us being apart for the longest spell so far. I took his solemn expression to mean that he had understood the significance of the day ahead. He sat on the floor and watched me as I sifted through my wardrobe searching through the elasticated cotton and tracksuits for something that would make sense. I pulled out storage bags full of my old work clothes feeling like I was rifling through a fancy-dress box and settled on something high-necked and black. Then I looked at myself in the mirror and laughed. I looked as shell-shocked and ridiculous as Marianne in that photograph taken in Ceylon. It was absurd. I left the baby with a sitter and tried to shake the feeling that I was venturing off on my own to some terrible fate.

We met at a restaurant beneath the railway arches. I followed him to the table and started talking, chatter so inconsequential that I could feel Marianne rolling her eyes. I had a glass of wine, I told stories, discussed the news, awkwardly at first but surprised at how quickly it felt natural again. We were both pretending, of course – that no conflict had ever existed and I hadn't been grey and dead behind the eyes when I left the office almost a year before. It was only now that I realised how angry I had been: angry with myself for failing and for failing to realise how hard it would be.

We still tiptoed around the big questions – are you coming back? Are you expecting to go part-time? The many other things he was thinking but wasn't allowed to say. I left him to wonder; my mind was made up. Wine-soaked and wobbly, I waved goodbye. 'I'll see you in a few weeks,' I said.

On the way home I looked out of the window as the train moved past high-rise apartments, old industrial units that had stood here almost as long as the train line. Virginia creeper had commandeered the structures, hanging down from the broken panes of glass like bright-red sails, the fluffy seed heads of clematis waving jauntily between like bearded mariners after many months at sea. I must have made this journey a million times and never really seen them before. I leaned my head against the cold glass window and tried to get my bearings again. Something had clicked; the world had slipped back on to its atlas and was moving in the right direction again.

I took Marianne's book out of my bag and started to read. She was growing frail now and her travelling days were coming to an end. Her final journey was to Chile, where she went to paint the monkey puzzle tree in its native habitat. When she got there, she was told that these oddities had disappeared in the hundred years since Archibald Menzies had been served the seeds on his dessert. That they had been sawn up and used as railway sleepers. Grimly determined, she succeeded in tracking one down; but this was a pattern that she had seen all around the world. Marianne had many flaws: she was a creature of empire, a man's woman who thought herself superior to other races and to her own sex, but she was attuned to the natural world around her in a way that was far ahead of her time. She could see that the world's resources were finite and that man was doing damage to the things she loved most of all.

In Tenerife she was distressed to see that the cochineal industry had destroyed the native wildlife – trees had been cleared away to plant the cacti for the insects instead. In California, where she travelled to see the coastal redwoods, she saw specimens fifteen feet in diameter and nearly 300 feet high being sawn up for firewood. 'It is invaluable for many purposes,' she wrote, 'and it broke one's heart to think of man, the great civiliser, wasting treasures in a few years to which savages and animals had done no harm for centuries.' Today those trees are classed as a vulnerable species. She was always more an observer than a collector, another way in which she differed from many botanists and hobbyists of the age. I could feel her dismay in South Africa when she saw a small group of aloes that grew over forty feet high and was told that Kew had 'coolly asked' for one to be cut down and a section sent to the museum.

Autumn had brought out the vulnerability of nature, and I noticed it as I got off the train and walked home. It was dark already, and with the energy of summer fading there was a frailty in the air. I walked past the statuesque London planes, their tangled branches stark against the dark sky, feeling intensely grateful to all the people I'd met, people who realised that plants were not here for our benefit – that we existed only because of them. This was the urgency that I had felt in Marianne's gallery, this was the message that she had understood and wanted to share. On the horizon I could see the familiar outline of my office, the building I would be returning to in a few weeks' time.

The lights stood out brightly in the evening darkness, and I felt excited to be going back there.

The next day the baby and I began the final phase of our mission. I wrapped him in a green snowsuit which covered him from top to toe and made him look like a small dinosaur. I strapped him to my front in his usual position, my shoulders objecting furiously to his weight. Then I checked that I had everything I needed for the day.

Instead of muslins and bottles I took secateurs and gloves. The baby and I set out to start retracing our steps around the parks near our home. In the few weeks since I had last been there the parched hillside near the almshouse was now a burnished bronze. I walked up, sweeping aside the fuzzy heads of the dried grasses, scouring like a hunter for his prey. Grasses came into their own in the autumn – some were lean and elegant with tasselled edges that blew in the breeze; others were short and jagged, sharp like miniature bamboos; each was brought to life by the wind. Balls of phlomis hovered in the air and the barbed, alien shape of teasel prepared its defences for the winter ahead. In between the bronzes and beiges of the plant skeletons there were flashes of colour, the vivid yellow of rudbeckia dancing gracefully above the squall. I placed the baby down on a rug and gathered a selection of acorns and sticks for him to play with. Then I got to work, collecting. It was an exercise in meditation, the quiet intensity of observing the wealth of life and material in one square foot of soil. I gathered translucent envelopes of honesty, pods of sea kale and puffy seed balls that look like miniature hot-air balloons. Each one was perfectly suited to its function.

There was an art to seed-collecting. The timing was essential. In some cases, like gorse, the casing exploded sporadically, a neat trick caused when the sun shone on the pod and made the water inside evaporate. You can hear them crackling on warm autumn days. I walked around each of the parks like a detective. Searching, doubling back when the coast was clear. It wasn't stealing, I told the baby, we were helping nature along the way.

The real stars of the autumn were the trees. I hadn't thought a great deal about them before, guiltily ignoring them as a whole other category that I would tackle another day. But at this time of year, when they formed a patchwork of colour, it was impossible to ignore them. I looked up at the red rowan, the brown oak, the yellow tulip tree, then waited for a gust of wind to blow the leaves to the ground. There was one that stood out; the *Ginko biloba* was small in size but spectacular, with fan-shaped leaves that looked as though they'd been carved from gold.

This was also the time to take cuttings, a pastime which gave me a Frankenstein-ish sort of thrill. We had studied this in our evening class, taking softwood clippings from sprigs of lavender, salvias and wallflowers under George's watchful eye. Then we stripped them all the way back to fragile twigs and planted them in their own little berths of soil. I practised at home with my houseplants, making a miniature philodendron by chopping off a stem and putting it in one of the old gripe-water bottles I had recycled as a vase. I liked to watch roots grow in water; it was hypnotic and sinister, like some sort of pickled oddity in an apothecary's shop.

Hardwood cuttings were the most mysterious of all. However many times George explained it, I never quite believed that you could snip off a branch, bare and inert, stick it in the earth and wait for a new tree to take root. Armed with this knowledge I became pathologically light-fingered. I snipped sprigs from the arcs of *Salvia 'Amistad'* I had admired all summer, swiped some sage from the herb garden at school. I took them home and put them in small pots of soil on the windowsills, with mini-incubators made out of freezer bags keeping them humid and warm. Until P surveyed the sitting room one evening. 'You've turned it into a greenhouse,' he said.

All of this collecting required a system of indexing. As the seeds I'd gathered lay on kitchen roll drying out, I sensed Linnaeus looking down upon my chaos with despair. Then I set about filling cupboards with envelopes, with newspaper pockets, in a semblance of order according to the parks they'd come from and when we would plant them back in the soil. The boys 'helped', lifting, sifting, losing towers of them down sofa cracks. While we worked indoors, winter slipped into the courtyard. Within a few weeks the acid-green leaves of my Japanese maple turned red and fell. The seed heads of the bronze fennel towered over the courtyard wall and the last of the erigeron daisies stooped their heads under the weight of the falling rain. The ferns, however, were in their element, relishing the refreshing downpours. It was a peaceful time, when life in my pocket garden decided to wind down. Only the mimosa hadn't got the message. If you looked carefully at the branches, you could already see balls of blossom beginning to take shape.

My last stop was the gated garden, which had rapidly become the boys' favourite place, a maze of dens where nettles grew knee-high and there was an endless choice of hiding places. I took them with me for the final task and got there late in the afternoon when daylight was beginning to fade. I pushed open the heavy iron gate and walked up the walled corridor to the open space within. The vermilion red of a Virginia creeper had carpeted one wall, twisting its way through the trees above, and turned the alley a brilliant pink. Plump red rosehips weighed down fragile branches, and the green hexagonal flowers of ivy struck out in new directions like antennae.

I noticed how run-down it looked – the tarmac was bumpy and uneven, one white wall had been cordoned off with red barriers by the council, the deep cracks running through it giving the impression that it might at any moment fall. I had been untangling the story of this garden. It was the final mystery I needed to solve, a last piece of the puzzle, but it turned out to be a vital one. The land at the top of the hill had once belonged to John Coakley Lettsom, a physician and botanist and this was the location of his house and ten-acre estate. He had been born on Tortola in the British Virgin Islands, where his family's wealth came from sugar plantations run on the labour of enslaved people. Lettsom was a Quaker and an early Abolitionist. On his father's death he freed the hundreds of slaves he had 'inherited' and returned to the island to work as a doctor.

He made money, returned to England and began encouraging others to liberate enslaved people as well. He founded the Medical Society of London and became a prominent campaigner for social reforms, including vaccinations. He published a treatise entitled *Diseases of Great Towns and the Best Means of Preventing them*, and opened up his gardens to people who lived nearby. He was also a passionate plantsman who financed plant-hunting expeditions to America and grew rare species here, alongside his orchards and greenhouses.

The scrubby patch of land that survived was saved from developers by local people who persuaded the council to lease it to them instead, and it had existed like this for decades. We got to the far end and turned back and there – for a just a moment – was a glimpse of what had been: a grand white manor house, set in rolling greenery, a bucolic scene. There was something heroic in that picture – a patch of land passed down through generations of strangers, an heirloom that busy, city-dwelling people had managed to keep.

Marianne's gallery opened on 7 June 1882. At this point there were 627 paintings on the walls and 246 pieces of wood, each from a different tree she had seen on her travels. She had started work on it the moment she unpacked her bags from a two-year trip around Australia. The building had been finished most satisfactorily in her absence and she now spent a year fitting and framing, patching and sorting her paintings. 'I had much trouble but also much pleasure in the work. What need now is there to remember the former?'

She intended to put an enlarged map of the world on the ceiling, 'coloured according to the geographical distribution of plants, in different shades of green and brown, the sea also shaded as it is in nature – clearest turquoise in the tropics, indigo in the middle seas, and green near the ice'. And she meant to include an index of fruits painted by herself on the cornice and twelve typical trees between the windows, 'but everyone was against such an unconventional idea,' she sighed. The wooden dado in particular caused headaches. Only half of the pieces 'came with names on them, and half were lost. It was a great difficulty to arrange them, but time mended all.'

Around the doors she had painted murals showing tea and coffee plants, a quiet barb to her friend Hooker for blocking her refreshment plans. He does not seem to have minded. In the official guide to the exhibition he wrote:

> very many of the views here brought together represent vividly and truthfully scenes of astonishing interest and singularity, and objects that are amongst the wonders of the vegetable kingdom and these . . . are already disappearing or are doomed shortly to disappear before the axe and the forest fires, the plough and the flock, of the ever advancing settler or colonist. Such views can never be renewed by nature, nor when once effaced can they be pictured to the mind's eye, except by means of such records as this.

The gallery cemented Marianne's renown as one of the three great Victorian lady adventurers, alongside Constance Gordon-Cumming, for whom she had often been mistaken ('we were both on a large scale'), and Isabella Bird, a rector's daughter who had started travelling on the advice of doctors as she suffered from numerous health complaints. Like Marianne, Isabella was a compulsive wanderer, visiting America, Australia and Hawaii, where she climbed the dormant volcano Mauna Kea, before opening a hospital in India. Marianne relates that soon after Miss Bird had finally accepted a marriage proposal, she was asked if she wouldn't like to visit New Guinea. She would have loved to, she said, but she was married now, 'and it was not the sort of place one could take a man'.

The three women came together in London for the very first time, and Marianne recounts how 'Miss Gordon-Cumming put her great hand on my shoulder at the same time, on which Lady A joined our three pairs of hands and blessed us – "three globe-trotteresses all at once!"'

I felt proud of her despite it all. I remembered the way I had felt standing in front of those paintings, the sensation of being clobbered over the head by all the world's parrots and plants. I could only imagine the impact it had on the crowds who came to see it then. One day, shortly after the opening, the gallery door was left open while Marianne was tinkering inside. A gentleman rushed in looking for Joseph Hooker and, finding her instead, asked: 'It isn't true what they say about all these being painted by one woman, is it?' It was true, she told him; in fact she had done it all herself. 'On which he seized me by both hands and said "Then it is lucky for you that you did not live two hundred years ago, or you would have been burnt as a witch."'

I I

Congelationis: The Month of Ice

It was dark when I opened the gate to the garden and made my way over the cobbled path to the schoolroom door in the dim glow of the street lights. Above me I could just make out the golden leaves of the wisteria twining around the pergola and getting ready to drop, while the lobed leaves of the chocolate vine were deep green and dappled in the cold night air. I stopped for a moment and inhaled the smells of the garden: the cold tang of winter combined with the heavy scent of mud. Somewhere in the distance someone was trying to light a fire. The smells were stronger now that I spent my days in an office, a sensory desert where the only sound came from the thrum of the air-conditioning vents. In the distance I could hear the Territorial Army practising their evening marches in the plot next door. The rustling in the bushes informed me that Flame the fox was present and correct.

A month into my old life and I was still surviving on adrenaline, coffee and prayers. I had felt so nervous preparing for the first day back that it took on a ceremonial feeling, like a Confirmation, a First Communion, a funeral perhaps. I got my hair cut apologising profusely to the lady whose job it was to sculpt something acceptable from the unruly mass I'd allowed to grow all year. Once more the bags had been brought up from beneath the bed and I rummaged through them, pulling out clothes I'd forgotten I'd ever owned and trying them on in front of the mirror as though resurrecting someone from the dead.

The practical preparation was the most intimidating of all. I had learned from the last time that reliable childcare was the stumbling block on which the whole enterprise could fall. So I started it all again, the nursery visits, the childminders, the balance between cost and care. Just as daunting were the gaping holes in my own knowledge. For twelve long months I had ignored the news agenda completely. I hadn't wanted to read about politics because I hadn't cared. I'd avoided newspapers in the supermarket, deleted social media accounts and flicked channels the moment the news came on. Now I would be catapulted back into the world of editorial conferences, pitching and arguing, of strong opinions when my own mind was serenely blank. For a journalist it was dangerous terrain.

I tried half-heartedly to catch up, attempting to engage P in the sorts of conversations we used to have, knowing that it wasn't really going to work because I didn't have anything to offer however hard I tried. I would have to wing it with a smile, just as Marianne had always done. The night before my first day back I walked around the house while P made supper, checking in on the aloe, the lemon tree, the orchid, which, miraculously, was still alive, with a new stem rising from the tangle of roots.

Winter was a precarious time for my indoor jungle, with temperatures dropping and the heating drying out the air. At least now I knew what to look for, how to read the plants' cries for help. A year ago I would have been oblivious as each one shrivelled and I probably wouldn't have cared. The next morning did nothing to soothe my fears. I walked through the glass doors of the office, where huge screens flashed up the most memorable front pages of the year. I realised that I hadn't read any of them and had forgotten what floor we were on.

The first few days passed in a whirl of polite conversation. Colleagues asked how the boys were and made gentle jokes about the relief of being back at work. I joined in, offering up platitudes and deflecting anything that might lead us to uncomfortable terrain. It felt odd to be back in this world of distant professionalism where colleagues were the people you saw every day but nothing of any real significance was ever said.

Perhaps no one had noticed the catastrophe that had taken place in front of them, the person who had left the office hollow and adrift? I sifted through the contents of my drawers as though rifling through the belongings of a stranger: a pair of high heels and a box of Tampax, which lay abandoned like the *Marie Celeste*. Only the news was familiar, the same churn of corruption, political scandal and abuse of power that weaved its way through life as the world turned. I sat at my desk with the TV news channels blaring above me and tried to figure out how and when to hop back on.

The early weeks were full of stops and starts, even with the childcare prepared and P on hand to help. Schedules went haywire, sleep regressed, the children caught bugs and their temperatures soared. I began to fret about things that hadn't happened and probably never would. Why was it that however quickly I moved, I never ended up in the right place?

From the office windows I could see across London Bridge to St Paul's and the City beyond. The view was impressive and inspiring, but it was a world that was almost entirely grey. Cut off from the courtyard, which I barely saw now that I left home and returned in the dark, I found myself itching more than ever for the soil. I missed greenery, craved it like an addict hankering for a hit. At lunchtimes I prowled around the streets, past overpriced food shops and chain restaurants where office workers came to sit in silence, their earphones in, on their lunch break. Eventually I found one solitary patch of green. Cross Bones Graveyard was one part of London that I was confident Marianne had never visited, a piece of unconsecrated land where prostitutes were buried until it was closed in 1853. Now there were multicoloured ribbons decorating the fence around it like a Buddhist shrine.

This too had been saved from development by campaigners and now there was a memorial garden inside, a tiny oasis where cascades of winter jasmine tumbled down the fence and yolk-yellow *Kerria japonica* exploded in mid-air. I sat on the bench and ate a sandwich, watching the dried heads of the hydrangeas softening the borders like antique lace.

The evening classes at the garden took on a new significance as the weeks wore on. I had agonised over whether or not to give up the course without finishing. I worried that the garden would be squeezed out of my life as it began to fill back up again, cast aside in the flood of new distractions like the heap of plastic toys that lay forgotten beneath the toddler's bed. Instead it had become more essential – the one appointment that I stubbornly refused to break. Every week I darted out of the office early, conjuring up ever more flamboyant excuses as I left meetings and jumped on to the first bus. This was my one non-negotiable fixture, the part of the week I simply wouldn't miss.

Now I walked up the paving knowing exactly what would greet me when I opened the classroom door. George, still in shorts despite the freezing weather, was perched on a Formica table, eating leftovers from a plate. Behind him there was a whiteboard full of squiggles: stolons and suckers, with barely decipherable explanations of how plants use these offshoots to spread. Richard gestured to the empty seat beside him and pushed over his folder full of scribbled notes. Dom nodded slowly in my direction, tapping the face of his watch as though to say, 'What kind of time do you call this?' This was a part of our routine now and Dom performed his role with joy; it was almost as funny to them as my office clothes.

Today it was a pair of high-waisted woollen trousers and a silk blouse. Good for interviewing authors, less so for digging up weeds. 'Sorry,' I mouthed as I crept round the back of the desks. I had thought that this, my final term, would be the least interesting. What was there to learn in winter when the ground was cold and so many of the plants were dead? There was no doubt that the mood of the garden had changed; the bananas were wrapped in blankets to protect them from the winter frosts and the echiums were melting like wax spires.

But just as some plants had come to an end, a whole new chorus was starting up. We put on our coats and traipsed out of the classroom by torchlight to see what we could find. The beds were full of life. Pink and purple cyclamens peered up from their striped zebra leaves, surveying the landscape, while a chorus of miniature pink trumpets sounded out from the viburnum, standing proud at the back of the bed. As I brushed past it the winter daphne enveloped me in the most delicious sugary smell.

Winter flowers have a particular desirability, a sophistication that their summer cousins lack. To make a garden beautiful in the summer is easy; to make it sing in winter requires real skill. Only connoisseurs recognised these touches: the delicate speck-led bells of clematis 'Freckles', a name which for once fitted, the fragile beauty of a crisp white hellebore, framed by dramatic spiked leaves. Winter flowers inspire devotion of a particularly obsessive sort. Snowdrops or *Galanthus*, from the Greek milk flower, for example, the bulbs already stirring beneath the soil, are the objects of fevered collecting. Galanthophiles have been coveting and trading these bulbs since soldiers brought them back at the end of the Crimean War. With their smallest porcelain lampshades heating up the February soil they were the humblest of flowers, but the most sought after could cost over a thousand pounds per bulb.

There were friendly ghosts in all corners of the garden. The clump of pampas grass that swept my head like a curtain reminded me instantly of Bev. In one corner of the vegetable bed was the chard I'd planted with Delphine, neon stems waving dark-green leaves. As ever, it was George's oddities that stole the show. On a table by the greenhouse sat an eerie beast, large spikes protruding from soft, furry leaves and orange and black fruit hanging below. It was a *Solanum mammosum* from South America, a distant relative of the tomato. Everywhere seed heads had been left standing like shadows to provide food and shelter for insects and birds. Their silhouettes formed shadows in the moonlight, jagged balls of echinops swirling like planets around the towering skeleton of the trumpet vine.

Winter wasn't a wasted season, it was essential for everything that came next. The bulbs beneath the soil needed the dark and cold to gather energy for the fireworks ahead. Just as we were about to go back inside, Ken let out a wail. He'd left his phone in one of the beds and it was on silent. Now dramatic moans filled the garden as we abandoned hopes of returning to the warm classroom. 'Careful, everyone,' George commanded, 'lift up the leaves, don't crush anything please,' as we began to rake through the beds.

I drifted into the greenhouse, grateful for an excuse to visit my favourite place. I still loved the smell and feel of this space, the hiss of machinery releasing steam into the air. It took me back to that first day at Kew; the scale was smaller but the effect it had on me was much the same, the delicate feathers of the eyelash fern, the fishbone cactus with its strange skeletal fronds. There were always new curiosities to inspect: the purple fur of the *Gynura aurantiaca*, or velvet plant, for example, brushing against the begonia's cheerful polka-dot leaves.

The colours and textures were so outlandish that they looked like drawings the toddler had done. The pathway in the middle was full of monstera leaves, bold and bullish as they pushed aside the fragile hearts of the Bodhi tree. It had been brought here for safe-keeping by a local Buddhist group, a cutting from the tree in India where Buddha achieved enlightenment, or so the story went and the responsibility for keeping it alive kept George in a state of perpetual fear. Beside it was the Victorians' favourite, the *Chamaedorea elegans*, known to Marianne and her peers as the parlour palm. I made my way to the heated propagator, which was full to the brim with tiny plants in pots. Some were sprinkled over with sparkling shards of light-reflecting vermiculite, their roots forming a complex network beneath the soil. They would be planted outside by another class in a few months' time. In a week or two I would have completed my diploma, the first qualification I had earned in almost twenty years. It would be utterly meaningless in the material sense; there would be no promotion or a pay rise because of it, but it felt more significant than any of that. It was proof that something had happened – that I'd discovered this garden and the people in it and the world had come into focus as a result.

At home, my own nursery still demanded attention. Plants lined the kitchen windowsills, where they could grab any passing rays of winter sun. Imperceptibly they grew bigger and stronger, their roots getting fatter as the winter wore on. It took all the power I could muster not to lift them from the soil and check their progress, to stick a finger in and poke around.

Next week was the baby's first birthday. Twelve months to the day since I lay back on that surgical trolley, lost and sick with dread. I could remember that, but almost nothing else from the first weeks of the baby's life. I scrolled through my phone and found one image of me holding him the night we came home. I'm grey but smiling and there he is curled into me, pale and terrified by his sudden ejection from dark to light.

We had been as fragile as each other, and Marianne had taken command. I had finished her book at last. As far as she was concerned her story ended when the gallery was complete. When she had hung the last paintings on the wall (she ran out of space and an additional panel was wheeled in to accommodate the last works) she settled down in Gloucestershire, a period she covers in her memoir in nine brisk lines:

I have found the exact place I wished for, and already my garden is becoming famous among those who love plants; and I hope it may serve to keep my enemies, the so-called nerves quiet for the few years which are left me to live. No life is as charming as a country one in England, and no flowers are sweeter or more lovely than the primroses, cowslips, bluebells and violets which grow in abundance all round here.

An epilogue written by her sister, Catherine, tells us more about what happened in her final years. Marianne devoted herself to her garden:

Kew sent her all sorts of foreign rarities, a fine collection of cistus, and splendid todeas for the fernhouse. All her florist friends Mr Wilson, Canon Ellacombe, Miss Jekyll [the famous garden designer Gertrude Jekyll] and many others sent generous contributions from their own famous gardens; all were very interested in her success. And how she worked! Every tiny plant, every bulb was put in with her own hand and under her own eye and every label was written by her . . . In the morning long before six, before her men were out of bed, she was out upon the lawn with the garden hose, patiently watering her fragile treasures.

She did not, however, get the peace she longed for. Catherine wrote that 'The enemy of her last two voyages – those weary, constant noises – never ceased. In the quiet of her country garden, as in noisy London, the overtired brain still translated these into human voices, whose words were often taunts.' She knew they were delusions, but still 'she suffered more than she owned, and dreaded being alone with those invisible but mocking foes', her sister said. Nor would it last. Marianne developed a disease of the liver and her health deteriorated. Catherine, who loved her but found her as baffling as most of her contemporaries did, observed that 'Her work was always her first point: for that she travelled, not to pass the time, as so many globe-trotters do in this age of easy locomotion. Her gallery at Kew is a monumental work: to finish it she fought bravely against increasing weakness; when it was done her strength was also gone, and the restful life she had dreamed of in her pretty Gloucestershire garden was not to be.'

She would finish the manuscript she'd been working on just before she died and call it *Recollections of a Happy Life*. Her publisher, John Murray, would reject it, complaining about the 'very great extent' of the manuscript and 'its most peculiar nature'. Never, he wrote, had he been so puzzled by a manuscript before. 'As far as I can conjecture the work, if printed, would extend to 3 or 4 volumes. Bringing it all out at once would,' he said delicately, 'I fear, prejudice its reception by the Public.' Marianne agreed that it could be cut and revised. She died that August, just as the flowers in her garden began to go to seed, but her sister would 'weed' her memoir for her and the first two volumes would be published in 1892.

So that was Marianne's ending, and now that I'd got there I felt disappointed, let down to discover that this force of nature had been fallible after all. Her sister wondered, as did I, whether she could really have enjoyed her quiet life in the English countryside.

Into the fifteen years immediately after her father's death had been compressed work sufficient for the lives of four ordinary women; and I have often wondered whether, if her strength had lasted another ten years, she could really have been content to sit down and wait for old age in the lovely green nest she had prepared for herself. Who shall say? She was a noble and courageous woman, whose like none of us shall ever look upon again.

She was right; Marianne was extraordinary for her time and for ours. She had challenged me to confront the world that I lived in and to understand the forces, for good and evil, which had shaped it. I put the books away on a shelf, grateful that I could take them down again if I ever needed to, but somehow doubting that I would. It was the world outside that she wanted me to notice. It was this that she had been directing me towards all the time: the trees and shrubs, flowers and leaves in the city, each one of them valuable and important, a net waiting to catch me if I fell.

Our story was written into them, and now I had a duty to protect them too. The baby was inscribed in the green spaces around us. Whenever I walked through the park by the hospital I could feel his fragile body, smell that delicious biscuit smell. With him I had travelled the globe, seen the forces that shaped it and met the people whose actions had brought us to this point in time. He had opened my eyes to a world full of extraordinary plants and courageous people, a universe I had never looked at properly before. Through him I had learned to notice the things that had seemed inconsequential before. He was the seed that started it all and I couldn't wait to watch him grow.

Epilogue

I am writing this looking out on the courtyard on a mild spring day. A lot has changed in the three years since this story ended, inside this garden and out. A global pandemic brought the world to a stop, making this small patch of space feel more precious than ever. Then, just as the virus was receding, my mother died.

She left us very suddenly and, having written a book about growing up, I now find myself feeling, more than ever, like a child. But I've had the opportunity to read these pages back, consider the events I've written about with the benefit of hindsight and see some things that I couldn't before. So I'd like to use this as a corrective. For a start, I am struck by how little of my mother there is in this book, which is misleading because even though she was away for quite a long period that year, she was on my mind an awful lot.

As I described, there was quite a long phase of my life when I was determined that I didn't want a family of my own. I liked my career. I liked my freedom. I resented the idea of sitting around, waiting to be wanted, only to find I was trapped and unable to leave again. I admitted this to anyone who was interested, including my mother, who paid no attention at all until I reached my late twenties, when it dawned on her that I might actually mean it. At this point she embarked on an intense and prolonged campaign to get me to change my mind.

When she had decided on a course of action, my mother had very little time for subtlety. There followed a period of angry diatribes, emotional guilt trips and evocative journeys into my lonely, barren future. On one occasion, she gave me a top with Chinese script down one side. 'What does it say?' my brother-in-law asked. 'It's an ancient Chinese proverb,' she said, casting a look in my direction. 'It means: Find man; have baby.'

I can't come up with one specific reason why this subject mattered so much to her, but I believe that motherhood was a core pillar of her identity. She loved her children, most children in fact, and was at her happiest when behaving like one. She had a seemingly endless appetite for pranks which she liked to play on those closest to her – dropping an apple core or an ice cube down your t-shirt on a hot day. She liked hiding things she knew you needed and watching gleefully as you hunted about getting more and more annoyed. I have lost track of the number of times I felt something landing on my head, only to find her, hands full of nuts, pebbles or some other missiles, shaking with mirth.

But she also knew first hand how precious life was. I am the youngest of my parents' four children. Their first, a little girl called Leila, was born with severe heart problems and died when she was six years old. I will never understand how my parents not only survived this but managed to create such a happy childhood for us as well. But somehow that is what they did. I know that this experience changed my mother and I would like to say that knowing that made me more tolerant of her campaign to make me procreate, but it did not. I bristled and retaliated in kind.

If you are reading this, you will know, of course, that I eventually caved. To her great delight, she got two more grandsons. The bickering between us stopped. Everything was all right. Until the baby was born, when suddenly it wasn't. The reason my mother is absent from this book is not because I didn't want to talk to her but because I couldn't. I was paralysed with fear that perhaps she had been wrong; that I wasn't cut out for this. Marianne, with her fondness for vegetables and her horror of domesticity, made me feel all right.

Things are very different today. The baby is no longer a baby; he is a big boy, he tells me with pride. He is fully fledged and articulate, so sure of himself that it is a constant battle to persuade him to listen to me at all. Only his hands are the same, sturdy hands, gardener's hands, I think as I watch him digging in the soil. I have been back at work for two years now. I returned with an open mind, willing to bow out if it became uncomfortable again. But this time it worked. I've thought a lot about why this is, but I think it is largely down to luck. That and a determination to be more honest. If people ask how it is going or what it was like, I tell them, even bringing the odd meeting to an abrupt halt with an unexpected flow of tears.

I have come to think of these jolts as aftershocks, tremors that I haven't yet managed to completely stop. I don't worry too much about it – I've been desensitised to shame.

Marianne taught me many things, but this was one of the most valuable. Unlike her, I have found that I can enjoy staying still. For the first time in my life, I am grounded in one place and I like it. It is a joy to watch the seasons playing out over and over again in the green spaces I know so well. People come and go: George has moved on; so has Bev. But cities are always changing and evolving; they are not supposed to stay still. The people who have cared about them leave their marks in the brickwork and traces of themselves in the parks. And while the grief I feel for my mother is acute, it isn't as disorientating as Marianne's.

When I did eventually tell her how bad things had been that year, she listened and she understood. And I realised what I hadn't when I was writing this book; that each of us fears at one time or another that we are not up to the job. My mother would have known that better than most.

Shortly after this, she began to arrive at the house with gifts. First it was three pots full of pure red geraniums. Then it was her plant bible, a battered old copy of Roy Lancaster's *Any Plant Any Place*, with pages folded and notes scribbled in the side. It turned out that my mother did love gardens and had been teaching herself about plants for many years. It became something we enjoyed together in the last two years of her life and a connection I'm very grateful for.

Though I miss her profoundly, I am comforted by the thought that this is the life she wanted me to live and she would want me to enjoy it. I don't know if this path will always lead to happiness. But I do know that, at this moment, my children are my greatest source of comfort. Their chaos is a distraction, their daily needs ease my own, and every now and then I get a glimpse of what feels like a miracle; sometimes, usually when they are misbehaving, I see a small flicker of her in them.

Acknowledgements

It is a strange thing to stand back and take stock of a story that has occupied your mind in one way or another for over three years and if I were to thank everyone who has played a part in getting me this far, this book would be even longer than Marianne's. However, there are a few people without whom it simply wouldn't exist. I owe a huge debt of gratitude to my agent, Sophie Lambert, who really did see potential in the least promising of places when I showed her the first jottings of an idea. She encouraged me to keep moving the building blocks around until they could stand up on their own. Thanks also to Maddy Price, my editor at Weidenfeld & Nicolson who under-stood exactly what it was that I was trying to convey and whose quiet wisdom has been invaluable throughout.

There would, of course, be no story to tell without the won-derful cast of characters I met over the course of a year. I have been struck over and over again by the generosity of those who took the time to get to know me, confided in me and ultimately trusted me to tell their stories. I hope you are not disappointed with the results. Thanks in particular to the team at Walworth Garden which more than anywhere became a home from home.

Not everyone I gardened alongside that year was able to give their consent to appear in these pages and in these cases I have taken steps to hide identities. If you do recognise yourself, I hope you are happy with the picture I have painted. On a practical level I could not have written or researched this book without the resources at the RHS Lindley Library and Kew Gardens, who have done such a wonderful job preserving Marianne's legacy all these years. My good friends Cal Flyn, Sara Hashash and Stephanie Tourbier have provided me with hours of free therapy and endless support through the experience of writing a memoir about a period of my life I would, in many ways, have rather forgotten. I hope I can return the favour one day.

It is undoubtedly my family who have suffered the most. P in particular, who guards his privacy almost as much as I disregard my own but who has always understood that this was something I needed to do. Thank you for your love and support, for juggling toddlers with such skill and for granting me the space to think.

We wouldn't have managed the past few years without the help provided by our wider families: parents and step-parents, brothers and sisters, all of whom rallied around, helping to feed and entertain my children on the countless occasions when I kicked them out of our home: thank you! My own parents deserve the greatest thanks of all – my father, who taught me to see beauty in language, and to my dearest mother, who gave me so much.

Finally, a note to my sons. Today, you are two tiny cyclones wreaking havoc on my life in new and exciting ways, but I know that one day you may want to read this book and that parts of it may be hard to get through. Please remember that the reason I wrote this story is because it is the only one that really matters: the one about how I met and fell in love with you.